LOVE@W

BY CORRIE JONN BLOCK, PHD, DBA

PASSIONPRENEUR®
PUBLISHING

LOVE@WORK

The Final Frontier of Empathy in Leadership

BY CORRIE JONN BLOCK, PHD, DBA

Publishing information
Publishing and design facilitated by Passionpreneur Publishing
A division of Passionpreneur Organization Pty Ltd
ABN: 48640637529

Melbourne, VIC | Australia
www.PassionpreneurPublishing.com

PRAISE FOR *LOVE@WORK*

With compelling stories and practical insights, *Love@Work* is a revolutionary book that challenges our ideas of how we love our colleagues, bosses, teams, and companies. Creating space for radical love in the workplace, Corrie equips you to foster inclusive environments, communicate effectively, and cultivate loving relationships that contribute to your personal and professional success. Whether you're a leader or someone looking for deeper purpose and relationships, *Love@Work* will transform your life and redefine the driving forces for your career.

—DR. MARSHALL GOLDSMITH
THINKERS50 #1 EXECUTIVE COACH AND NEW YORK
TIMES BESTSELLING AUTHOR OF *THE EARNED LIFE,
TRIGGERS,* AND *WHAT GOT YOU HERE WON'T GET YOU THERE*

Corrie is a genuinely loving leader, and *Love@Work* is a timely and critically needed addition to the expert toolkit for empathy, trust, and inspiration in leadership. One of the best ways to create trust is to show that you genuinely care about and love people. If trust is what adds speed to teams and organisations, then caring and love are what add strength to trust.

—STEPHEN M. R. COVEY
THE NEW YORK TIMES AND #1 WALL STREET JOURNAL BESTSELLING
AUTHOR OF *THE SPEED OF TRUST* AND *TRUST & INSPIRE*

A rare gem among leadership literature, as it fearlessly delves into the concept of love in a platonic and professional context. Corrie's presentation of these principles is among the most comprehensive and actionable that I have come across. He masterfully elevates the conversation around leadership, challenging us to step into our roles with a deep sense of care, compassion, and love. By the time you reach the final page, you will be equipped with the tools, insights, and inspiration to create work cultures that foster love, connection, and ultimately, greatness.

—MARK C. THOMPSON

WORLD'S #1 CEO COACH

Corrie is a focused and dedicated individual who consistently inspires those around him. His work ethic is truly impressive, and he is a great role model for anyone looking to excel in their career. Working with him has been a pleasure, and I would recommend him to anyone without hesitation.

—JOHN SANEI

FUTURIST AND BEST-SELLING AUTHOR OF *WHAT'S YOUR MOONSHOT?*

One of the greatest gifts that we can give to others is the experience of feeling trusted, appreciated and loved. And when this is part of the culture within the teams that we lead, we are able to unleash the potential that resides within us all. This book shows us why this matters and how we already have what it takes to transform our work environment for the better.

—SIMON ALEXANDER ONG

BEST-SELLING AUTHOR OF *ENERGIZE*

Dr. Corrie Block is the world's leading authority on the important subject of making business personal. I've read all his previous books and there are exceptional nuggets within each chapter. I'm really excited for *Love@Work*, and I believe it will be the new benchmark on loving leadership.

—ADAM ASHCROFT

THE ADVANTAGE COACH AND

BEST-SELLING AUTHOR OF *THE ADVANTAGE PLAYBOOK*

I loved this book! Our working world has never faced so much disruption from AI, automation, and robotic technologies so as we head into the future it's more important than ever that we focus on and promote human strengths and human values and create workplaces that are filled with empathy and the human emotions that make humankind unique.

—MATTHEW GRIFFIN

FOUNDER & CEO, 311 INSTITUTE AND XPOTENTIAL UNIVERSITY

A brilliant and insightful read on why it's time to go BIG on human-centred leadership and empathy as a central workplace pillar.

—TERRENCE MAURI

HACK FUTURE LAB FOUNDER AND BEST-SELLING AUTHOR OF *THE 3D LEADER*

An addictive and engaging narrative that captivates readers from start to finish. *Love@Work* should be mandatory reading for executives at all levels. It underscores the crucial role leaders play in creating an environment that enables employees to thrive. Dr. Block's storytelling prowess and his ability to connect with readers across cultures makes this book an invaluable resource for anyone striving to create positive change in their workplace.

RON THOMAS

MANAGING DIRECTOR, STRATEGY FOCUSED GROUP

Love@Work delivers a refreshingly real and sustainable approach to humanised leadership while also providing reassuring answers to the questions leaders are often hesitant to ask. Dr. Corrie challenges your self-awareness, inspires you to be better, and sets a new, healthy, and progressive standard for empathetic leadership.

—AHMAD IMAM

FOUNDER AND CEO, THE EXECUTIVE BRAND

Having known Corrie for over five years now and actively following his thought leadership, his new book exploits hard questions which as company owners is only a challenge of focus. Corrie has been for many years a leader in the Middle East in this field, and this is another example of him showing us what we know, through his new book *Love@Work*.

—STEVE MAYNE

SERIAL ENTREPRENEUR

An area of leadership not often addressed and yet so important is being treated here. Corrie has done a great job setting the parameters to discuss what love is in the workplace and what it isn't. A very important contribution.

—HANS CHRISTENSEN

MANAGING DIRECTOR, KENSTON BUSINESS

The pandemic revealed the power of intangibles. Probably the most important one is empathy. Leaders showed empathy, and HR teams promoted empathy, which made a difference in how people adapted and thrived. *Love@Work* is one of the best treatments on the use of empathy in the workplace.

—JACK PHILLIPS

CHAIRMAN, THE ROI INSTITUTE

Love@Work is a subject that people talk way too little about. It doesn't matter if you're the leader of a company or if you've just started your career. There are plenty of takeaways for all who want to develop as a leader (or even as a human) in this book.

—MAGNUS TOVEBERG
EXECUTIVE DIRECTOR, DANIEL WELLINGTON

Love@Work is a magnificent piece of work. I genuinely appreciate the fresh approach, and that none of the topics are clichéd, which is remarkable given that empathy is a well-explored subject.

—CHRISTIAN FARIOLI
CEO & DIGITAL MARKETING LECTURER AND BEST-SELLING AUTHOR OF *THE PIZZA GUIDE TO DIGITAL MARKETING*

Love@Work is a profound and transformative guide on my journey towards becoming a better leader. Dr. Corrie's insights, personal experiences, and compelling anecdotes truly spoke to my heart. If you are seeking to lead with empathy, build meaningful relationships, and create a harmonious work culture, this book will deeply resonate with you.

—DANIEL STOJANOVSKI
CEO, TRANSFORM DIGI

Corrie Block is a thought leader, author and business coach who ensures optimum performance with accountability for leaders globally, and delivers results.

—GAUTHAM GANGLANI
CEO, RIGHT SELECTION GLOBAL THOUGHT LEADERS

Love@Work is an engaging read that grapples with the most confusing human element – love – and its role in the context of building great organisations. Corrie's ability to paint vivid imagery through his story telling and transparency, backed by scientific research, makes the read compelling and thought provoking. Highly recommended for leaders at all levels for its impact on all aspects of life.

—AVANTIKA GUPTA

FOUNDER AND CEO, CARVE INTERIORS

Love@Work is the seminal text on love in leadership. I've known Dr. Corrie for a few years now and I am proud to say that he lives what he writes. Every leader should read this.

—LORENZO JOORIS

CEO, CREATIVEZONE

Dr. Corrie Block's views on leadership have had a tremendous impact on me and have reaffirmed my belief that the world of business is indeed personal. We are meant to bring purpose and meaning to what we spend half our lives doing, that there is no work-life balance because it's all LIFE, and we can't lead and inspire others if we're not operating from peak performance habits that make us excel in business and in life. Corrie's work continues to challenge and inspire me to up my game and play full out. Eternally grateful for his mentorship and friendship!

—SHEREEN QUTOB

DIRECTOR OF TALENT MANAGEMENT & CULTURE, MAJID AL FUTAIM

I highly recommend *Love@Work*. Throughout my career I have always had a profound connection and genuine care with the people I worked with but never knew it had an impact on results until I read this book. It provides real-life examples from Corrie's experience that I truly relate to, as well as insightful perspectives on leadership and the influential role of love.

—AHMED ATWI

SERIAL ENTREPRENEUR AND FOUNDER OF LAVA HOSPITALITY

I love the context and I find it super important to bring love to work. I enjoyed Dr. Corrie's personal stories and I'm sure many leaders will benefit from reading this.

—NIOUSHA EHSAN
CEO, LINKVIVA EVENTS

This book handles a simple concept we are originally born with in our innate nature, addresses how far and complicated we are from this nature, and helps clear the way to bring you back. It has given me the courage to be, create, and radiate love at work, at play, with friends, in meetings, on the road, in life.

—VARUN HINGIRANI
DIRECTOR, TAGIT RFID SOLUTIONS

Dr. Corrie is my go-to when it comes to understanding the latest science around executive health and performance. We work exclusively with businesspeople and as such his support and guidance has been extremely helpful.

—CAMERON HARRIS
FOUNDER, TRUTH FITNESS

I LOVE this book! Through humor and facts Dr. Corrie challenges the norm of leadership in what is increasingly a multi-cultural workplace that deserves to adapt.

—PHIL BEDFORD
THE REBEL NETWORKER AND MANAGING PARTNER AT ASENTIV

For many years I have been in awe of Dr. Corrie's complete knowledge of business and the leadership psyche. Very few so-called experts address the most challenging situations that decision-makers face in a modern workplace and provide such simple, implementable solutions that elicit realistic tangible outcomes in the shortest possible time. He's the real deal and in my opinion sits alongside Simon Sinek, Marshall Goldsmith and Jack Canfield in his mastery of thought leadership and business analysis. His latest book *Love@Work* provides insights to some of the biggest problems that face entrepreneurs and managers in the post-pandemic era and should be bought, shared and consumed immediately by every leader who wants a greater level of control over their future successes.

—DAVE CRANE

CEO, THE GAME CHANGERS AND INTERNATIONAL KEYNOTE SPEAKER

Boldly humane, relatable, and an easy-to-read book. Love at work is often taken for granted, misinterpreted, and ignored, leading to devastating consequences, and missed opportunities. This book provides a new way of examining the redemptive power of empathetic and loving relationship/ leadership at work and its profound implications on factors such as reciprocal responses and interaction, positive social cohesion, meaningfulness, inclusion, job satisfaction, performance, and returns on investment.

—PROF. RAYMOND LIHE

SENIOR LECTURER IN STRATEGY AND

BUSINESS ANALYSIS, DE MONTFORT UNIVERSITY

A very brave and thought-provoking book. Once again, Corrie shows himself willing to tackle important issues head-on. He forces his readers to re-think workplace dynamics. This book upturns the main structure of the workplace, and places the people and their interaction at the heart of a successful workplace environment. Many might believe they understand "love" and its place in our lives. This excellent book challenges that understanding by extending that thinking and throws "love" right onto every desk and boardroom table.

—JEFFREY FARROW

SERIAL ENTREPRENEUR AND ANGEL INVESTOR

This book is a refreshing read that confidently discusses *Love@Work* – pushing boundaries and challenging readers to explore how passion is more than being dedicated to your job, emphasising the need for emotional and psychological connection in the workplace. It puts the spotlight on how leaders have the responsibility to assure the welfare of their team. Corrie offers his personal experiences and research in a fun and intelligent way. You'll really begin to ask yourself, "What's the loving thing to do?"

—HARMEET SINGH

DIRECTOR, AL MASAOOD GROUP

Dr. Corrie provides a profound perspective on love and empathy, demonstrating how these qualities develop meaningful relationships that can facilitate in transforming workplaces into caring environments. A compelling read that will transform the way we approach the power of love in professional settings.

—MOHAMED MARICAR

DIRECTOR, BANIYAS BUILDING MATERIALS CO.

One of the best trainers and a great coach. Dr. Corrie is inspiring and supportive. Besides being one of my best friends, Dr. Corrie is great advisor and has helped me a lot from the creation of my company to all business aspects. I believe it's not only his knowledge and experience, it's his personality and character that really creates positivity in those around him.

—WALID DHAFER

CEO, UNIGLOCAL INTERTRADE

Love@Work has been a wonderful read. Dr. Corrie's expertise and deep understanding of love and leadership offers a fresh perspective on how these two elements can coexist and amplify each other in the workplace. This book has challenged me to reevaluate my approach to leading, and I genuinely believe I will be a better leader for it.

—HOLLY CASARES

DIRECTOR OF TALENT AND PERFORMANCE, SHORY

Love@Work has created a new space in my mind, allowing me to hear the echoes of thoughts that validate the love that I am made of, embrace my weaknesses, value all kinds of love, and navigate my path in life.

—LEILA KANTAR
BUSINESS DEVELOPMENT MANAGER, AL MASAOOD GROUP

What Corrie describes in *Love@Work* is the essence of life, not only business. Nothing is worth doing if it is not done with love. So why should we exclude love from our business relationships? Being heart centric is at the essence of humanity and we should not artificially separate between our basic existence as loving creatures and our professional existence. Every single page in this book is worth reading, because it has been written with love – I know that for sure, because that's how Corrie is: an empathetic and loving human being!

—MUHAMMAD CHBIB
SERIAL ENTREPRENEUR

TABLE OF CONTENTS

For my five beautiful children:
Gabriel, Grace, Harrison, Piper, and Levi.
Imagine a more loving world, then build it around you.

ACKNOWLEDGEMENTS

I've been reading, writing, teaching, and learning leadership for three decades. I'm grateful to influential researchers and writers who came before me, including:

Barry Pozner	John Maxwell	Peter F. Drucker
Henry Mintzberg	Max De Pree	Robert House
James M. Kouzes	Marshall Goldsmith	Simon Sinek
Jim Collins	Patrick Lencioni	Stephen M. R. Covey

I have read hundreds of books on leadership, and thousands of research articles. It would take another whole book to acknowledge all of those published authors who have influenced my thinking on leadership over the years. Thank you all for sharing your thoughts with me. I've heard you.

I'm also grateful for the influence of lesser-known leaders who have poured their wisdom into me as I continued to develop my ideas over the last three decades:

Ago Lilleorg

Ahmad Imam

Brent Cantelon

Darcy & Leanne McAlister

Dave Crane

David Boyd

Dawn Block

Ernie & Joni Block

Ian Netton

JJ & Rachel Starky

Joyce Reece

Kory & Heather Sorensen

Mart & Alta Vahi

Mihkel & Veronika Madalvee

Moustafa Hamwi

Meiraj Hussein

Murray Cornelius

Randy & Judy Sohnchen

Rod & Kaja Corcoran

Scott Benstead

Walid Dhafer

I'm certain there are many more that have escaped my mind right now, but perhaps it's enough to say that we are all in some way the products of the meaningful conversations we have had with those around us who influence us, and I am eternally thankful to all of you who have influenced me.

More recently, I have learned more about leadership from my coachees than anyone. In the capacity of coach to leaders in organisations, from start-ups to multinationals, I continue to learn from the challenges and opportunities, puzzles and ideas of those whom I am privileged to serve as a business coach and executive coach. Thank you to all of you for your collective wisdom.

Thank you as well to my covenant partner and best friend, Nicole, without whom I could neither have written this book, nor achieved any of what I've attempted in the last number of years. You are my other self, Dcukie.

FOREWORD

By Mark C. Thompson, World's #1 CEO Coach

The responsibility for cultivating work cultures that encourage the hearts and minds of our employees rests squarely on the shoulders of us as leaders. It is a weighty responsibility, but one that is crucial for creating workplaces that inspire and uplift. In this book, *Love@Work*, we are presented with an invaluable roadmap for achieving exactly that.

What sets this leadership book apart is its unique blend of scientific evidence and captivating storytelling. It seamlessly weaves together research and real-life examples, making a compelling case for the transformative power of love in the workplace. Personally, I found myself deeply resonating with Corrie's five-step process for fostering connectedness within organisations. The approach is refreshingly clear, practical, and, above all, desperately needed in today's fast-paced and often disconnected corporate environments.

In my own work as a coach, I have built a foundation rooted in trust and transparency, principles that Corrie eloquently discusses throughout the book. I have always believed that breaking through the formalities of professional distance and forging genuine connections with my clients on a heartfelt level is essential to their growth and success. Although it may not always be explicitly expressed, I am well aware that I perform at my best when I truly care for my clients. As a coach, my ultimate goal is to help them lead better lives, and it is in this realm of open minds and open hearts that, as Corrie wisely counsels, we experience greater happiness, improved wellbeing, heightened effectiveness, inclusivity, and even greater financial success.

Love@Work is a rare gem among leadership literature, as it fearlessly delves into the concept of love in a platonic and professional context. Corrie's presentation of these principles is among the most comprehensive and actionable that I have come across. He masterfully elevates the conversation around leadership, challenging us to step into our roles with a deep sense of care, compassion, and love. It is a call to action that resonates deeply with me, and I am thrilled to be in a career where I can join Corrie in encouraging other leaders to embrace these transformative principles for themselves and their teams.

As you embark on this journey through *Love@Work*, prepare to be inspired, enlightened, and challenged. Corrie expertly guides us through a transformational exploration of what it truly means to lead with love. By the time you reach the final page, you will be equipped with the tools, insights, and inspiration to create work cultures that foster love, connection, and ultimately, greatness.

Together, let us embrace the power of love in leadership and cultivate workplaces where hearts and minds can truly thrive.

INTRODUCTION

I'd like to share a very awkward conversation that I had with a client a couple of years ago. He was the CEO of a company for which I was providing strategy consulting. I had been working with him closely for a few months, and I called him one day to discuss a few of my recommendations that he wanted to execute.

We talked for about twenty minutes, mostly about the impact of my recommendations on key employees who might feel marginalised or devalued if we didn't execute them well. I could tell that he was committed to the change, but genuinely worried that his people might feel hurt in the process. It was an emotive and mutually empathetic discussion between two professionals.

At the end of the conversation, we agreed on a communications strategy that would help mitigate potential feelings of devaluation in those whose job roles we wanted to change. I thanked him for his transparency and openness to change, and I applauded the care and concern he had for his team. Then in a completely unprofessional and totally uncalculated move, I ended the conversation with, "Ok, let's talk more on Monday. Bye. I love you."

My heart stopped.

Did I just tell my CEO client that I love him? My eyes widened in panic and my thumb scrambled to find the big red button on the screen to end the call as quickly as possible. I needed to cut the connection before he could say anything. But it was too late, I didn't make it in time. I heard his voice as I lowered my phone, equally casual, equally uncalculated as he replied,

"Ok. Love you too."

And that was it. I hung up.

We never spoke of it again.

But why not? Of course, it was a slip of the tongue, but why can't I tell him I love him? Did the nature of our relationship as professionals really disqualify us from loving each other? Here's my current frustration:

> *IT DOESN'T MAKE SENSE TO ME THAT THE HIGHEST POTENTIAL QUALITY OF HUMAN RELATIONSHIP (LOVE) IS INTENTIONALLY EXILED FROM THE PLACE WHERE WE SPEND THE MOST TIME WITH OTHER HUMANS (WORK).*

LOVE IS FOR ALL PEOPLE

What if you could improve the quality of life for yourself and others in absolutely every human interaction you have, especially those in your place of work, would you want that?

Would it improve the quality of your life if you felt heard at work, and know that you were understood, valued, and truly loved?

It's important to note that the needs and concerns I'll address in this book are intrinsic to all people, including you. But there are eight billion voices wanting to be heard in the world, and yours is just one of them. There are also eight billion opportunities for you to love, and to feel truly loved.

As a leader in your organisation, how can you improve the quality and impact of your influence on others by helping them to feel heard, understood, valued, and loved by you?

I want you to imagine your followers, listeners, employees, friends, and colleagues all feeling this way when they interact with you. How would that improve the effectiveness of your leadership? How might that impact the speed and accuracy with which you reach your shared goals as a community? How would your life improve as a result of becoming better at leading, through a progression of listening to loving those around you?

> **THIS BOOK APPLIES TO EVERY PERSON, BUT IT IS PRIMARILY WRITTEN FOR LEADERS IN ORGANISATIONS.**

This book applies to every person but is primarily written for leaders in organisations. For ease of reading, I'll use the words leader, manager, and boss interchangeably. I am aware of the distinctions between these three role titles and the kinds of influence they represent, but that's not the focus here. All the materials apply equally to those who call themselves leaders, managers, and bosses.

Whether you're an entrepreneur in a start-up, or a CXO in a multinational corporation, organisational leaders are surrounded by people who all have the same basic desire: to be loved. My aim here is to tap into that psychological need and provide practical tools for efficient and effective communication; they will offer previously unrealised benefits for you as a leader, and for your economic community (your company).

LEADERSHIP IS FOR EVERYONE

I'm writing this book in a humble attempt to fill a gap I see in professional leadership, the one between respect and love. This gap might be labelled "professional distance." This is a term I don't like at all. I think it has done at least as much damage as good in our business contexts.

Professional distance encourages people to hold each other at arm's length instead of in each other's arms, the latter of which I find more and more wanted and needed in our increasingly complicated, individualistic, dehumanised and commoditised career contexts.

Ultimately, I want us to connect with each other better, to believe in each other more, and to recognise in each other the value that we all add to the world in the work that we do every day. I believe that each person on this planet has a sacred responsibility to our human community to add value through our work. Work is an expression of gratitude for the abundant world in which we were born.

My work is my act of gratitude for the ten thousand generations of successful human lives that led to the connected and abundant world in which I now live, and I'm not about

> **WORK IS AN EXPRESSION OF GRATITUDE FOR THE ABUNDANT WORLD IN WHICH WE WERE BORN.**

to let the momentum of centuries of economic and political peacemaking be hijacked in my generation by dehumanising business principles.

So ... can we love each other at work?

That's the guiding question of this book, and the answer as I hope you'll soon agree, is ... YES!

WHAT YOU CAN EXPECT

By the end of this book, you'll:

- Understand why love is excluded from workplace conversation;
- Learn the history and meaning of professional distance;
- Define what it means to love and be loved in the workplace;
- Learn to apply love and loving leadership at work;
- Clearly define the difference between love and romance;
- Learn how diversity, equity, and inclusion are just the beginning of love at work;
- Learn how to truly hear others around you;
- Help others around you to feel understood;
- Recognise when you are valued;
- Actively pursue loving relationships with your colleagues and employees.

I'm coming at this from a long history in organisational leadership. I started working at McDonald's when I was fourteen years old, more than thirty years ago. Since then, I have started five successful businesses of my own and have provided leadership training and executive coaching in more than 150 companies worldwide.

I am currently one of the leading business coaches in the Middle East and a widely recognised management and leadership expert (or so I'm told). My academic interest in love at work stems from my role as a Professor of Strategic Management, although I'm going to try to keep this book accessible to all readers.

CHAPTER CONTENT

Each chapter has stories that will help you connect with the concepts and make them easier to understand. I'll include reviews of scientific research that provide evidence for the concepts introduced in each chapter as well.

I'm a storyteller, but I'm also a science writer. I've tried to balance the need for strong scientific backing with a desire that this book be easily read and understood by leaders and managers in professional organisations. I hope I've achieved this.

At the end of each chapter, I've included a cheat sheet for you in two sections: First Principles and Next Steps.

First Principles are the big ideas from each chapter that you will want to keep in mind. Each of them is mapped back to where the concept occurs in the text, so it's easy to find later. For example,

"**FP5.3**" – translates to: First Principle, Chapter 5, Number 3.

I've also included all the First Principles in an appendix at the back of this book. If you recall a concept later and want to return to it, this appendix will make it easier to find. Next Steps are my suggestions for how you can implement the learning from that chapter into your life and leadership. I have tried to make them as universal as possible, but you'll need to decide for yourself which ones you are willing and able to implement.

The back of the book also includes a Further Reading list, which contains a number of sources that have influenced my thinking on this subject, but which I did not interact directly with in the book. It's for academics like me that really want to head down the rabbit hole academically. Feel free to ignore it.

THIS BOOK IS HIGHLY "UNPROFESSIONAL"

It might be considered unprofessional for you to step into your boss' office exclaiming, "I love you." That's the kind of soft skill that isn't encouraged at work (yet). So, a quick word of caution if you are thinking that this is a soft skills book: it's really not.

There's absolutely nothing "soft" about love. As you'll see, love is challenging. It requires effort. It takes a considerable invest-ment of time and energy to achieve and can be devastating when lost. This is a hard book on hard skills. Difficult to accept, challenging to learn, and nearly impossible to master.

If you're looking to be cuddled into thinking that you should be loved as a leader "just as you are" then you're reading the wrong book. And if you're looking for a quick fix for bad lead-ership, you've definitely come to the wrong author for advice. It would be better for you to listen to a couple of positive psychology podcasts and read a blog written by some CEO's ghostwriter. That direction will probably make you feel better.

This is also not a book about loving *what* you do for work. If you want to love the actual activities you do at work and connect better to your work that way, I recommend you read *Love + Work* by Marcus Buckingham.[1]

In this book, we'll tackle the driving forces behind what makes us feel connected to each other as humans and apply them to our organisations. We'll start with the beginning of connection – feeling included – and culminate in the foundational elements of love: loyalty, service, and self-sacrifice.

I am aware that it sounds unprofessional to say that we should pursue and experience love at work, or that we, as leaders, can learn to lead in a way that helps our people to enjoy that experience. However, I've never been a big fan of the status quo, and I suspect that true reciprocity in this idea will lead to a new competitive edge in our increasingly competitive business contexts.

So, are you ready to get a bit unprofessional with me?

---

1   Buckingham, M. (2022). *Love + work: How to find what you love, love what you do, and do it for the rest of your life.* Harvard Business Review Press.

INCLUDED, HEARD, UNDERSTOOD, VALUED, AND LOVED

CHAPTER 1

NAVIGATING LOVE

An Overview of How We're Going to
Tackle This Beast of a Topic

"LEADERSHIP WITHOUT LOVE IS MANIPULATION."

—RICK WARREN, *THE PURPOSE DRIVEN LIFE*

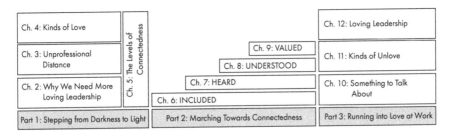

FIGURE 1:   THE LOVE@WORK ROADMAP

In this chapter I'll give you an overview of the whole book, so you can see where we're going and why. But first, let's start with a bit of talk on love.

TO LOVE IS TO BE HUMAN

I was raised to understand love as the most powerful state of any human relationship – between parents and their children, between spouses and partners, or between best friends for life. I am blessed to have known, and to continue to abide deeply in, all of these kinds of loving relationships. I hope you are too.

As a child, I related primarily with people I was loved by and could appropriately love in return. Friends, my siblings and parents at home, the people at church who were told all the time to "love one another," and my teachers at school. What I wasn't taught was this: when I grew into an adult, I was going to have to spend half of my life in a job, with people I wasn't supposed to love. And if I did in fact end up loving any (or all) of the people I worked with in my career, I definitely shouldn't tell them so. That would be inappropriate.

It never felt quite right to me that the richest, most meaningful, most powerful form of human relationship (love) is something that we actively exclude from a domain of relationships that occupies so much of our lives (work).

Why would we do that? Why can't we (shouldn't we?) pursue and express loving relationships in the workplace, and especially as leaders who aim to improve the quality of the lives of our people?

I have long believed that your work is:

1. Not just a job, but is half of your life: you have a limited number of days on this planet, so anything that comprises half of every day should be as meaningful as possible;
2. An exchange of value: you are adding value to society in exchange for a share of that society's resources, which you can in turn trade for other things; and
3. A fundamental expression of gratitude: you were born into an abundant world, full of technology, healthcare, and opportunities that you didn't create. Contributing your efforts to making the world better is how you express your gratitude.

We have so much to be grateful for. In spite of current unsolved and arising challenges, we are living in the most prosperous, abundant, and peaceful time in all of human history.[2] We are not where we should be yet, but we're definitely not where we were a thousand or even a hundred years ago, either. Although pain, violence, and injustice still exist in our slowly improving world, the default world that our next generations are being born into is better than it was when we were born.

I think that the proper response to our existence is gratitude. And if we can agree that gratitude is an appropriate starting place for being alive, then perhaps love is a more accessible and attainable goal for living.

---

2   Pinker, S. (2012). *The better angels of our nature.* Penguin.; Diamandis, P. H., & Kotler, S. (2014). *Abundance.* Free Press.

But I struggle with love.

It's complicated, powerful, emotive, and sometimes really messy. My first wife and I divorced after 22 years of marriage, and although I was deeply in love with her for a quarter of a century, the love I had for her dramatically changed. I then fell in love with my second wife Nicole. I still deeply love my high-school best friend, Joey, although living on opposite sides of the world means we only see each other every couple of years.

I have loved all kinds of people who have crossed my path as friends, sometimes for a little while and sometimes for years. And then there are the enduring loves I have for my parents and my five children that seem to transcend all other kinds of love. But even in its most powerful or enduring forms, as with my children, I have not always been very good at communicating love.

INCLUDED, HEARD, UNDERSTOOD, VALUED, AND LOVED

I remember when my older children were young, all they wanted was my attention. Sometimes it was to ask a question or show me something they found interesting. Often it was just to share something they'd just learned about the world and wanted me to know as well. Whatever it was, they needed my attention, and I was not great at giving it to them, at least that's my memory of it.

Often, my first wife, Dawn, and our two kids, Gabriel and Grace, would accompany me as I travelled and spoke on stages around the world. I had a very public life, and so my time was shared with lots of people who wanted my attention. Our family dinners were often shared with clients, followers, employees, partners, and others interested in discussing things with me.

I remember lots of times stepping off the stage and into a crowd of people eager to connect with me. Not wanting to be aloof or unapproachable, I would do my best to listen to each one and connect with them, just trying to add a small bit of value to their lives during our brief interactions. My own children were often two of those interested people. At the time, this felt more like an interruption than an important interaction.

My kids would approach me while I was with the grown-ups to ask me mundane things like "can we go now?" or "do you know where my toy is?" The answer of course was always: no and no. We couldn't go now, and I didn't know where their toys were.

I was annoyed. But much more meaningful than my irritation with them was their steadily growing sense of how unimportant they were to me at those times. They learned not to expect my attention, or to expect an unfavourable response if they somehow managed to get it.

But I'm only human, right? I couldn't listen to both the curious and engaging stranger in front of me and the childhood concerns of my kids. I had to choose. Someone was going to be ignored by me. Someone was going to feel unheard.

My son was about six years old, and my daughter was two when I finally figured this all out and realised what my lack of response was communicating to them. They didn't know the rules of adult conversation or understand that interrupting one was considered impolite in the grown-up world. They didn't value the limited time I had with these strangers, or my excitement at having my ideas valued and discussed by them.

I remember being in the lobby after speaking at an event, and my son was visibly upset that I had ignored his attempts to hijack my attention. I was annoyed and he was hurt. So I designed a small but very important ritual that my kids used from that day onward. I knelt down and made eye contact with my six-year-old boy, recognising his feelings of being marginalised, isolated, and excluded.

I said, "I love you, Gabriel. I'm sorry that I ignored you. What can I do for you?" And after looking at the drawing he had made and telling him that he had done a great job, I asked him, "Would you please help me with something?"

Of course, he was eager to help. He was a loving child who only wanted to matter to his super-hero father.

"When Daddy is talking with adults, sometimes what they are talking to me about is very important to them, and they really need me to listen to them and try to help them. And I know that at those times you sometimes also need me to listen to you and help you, too. So when you see that I'm listening to someone else and you need me to listen to you, please come to me and put your hand on my leg. I will notice that you are there, and as soon as I can, I will stop talking to the other person and I will talk to you. Can you do that for me?"

And he did.

From that day onward, I often found myself in small crowds of people, in meetings, or at a dinner table discussing something meaningful only to adults, when I would feel a tiny but unmistakable hand gently touch my thigh. It remained there for as long as required, often several minutes, silently reminding me that he was in line for my attention.

And as soon as it was socially acceptable, I would excuse myself from the conversation to kneel down and hear his question, concern, or idea. And Gabriel taught his younger sister to do the same. I began to anticipate that hand on my leg. The kids were patient, silent, and calm; although I would make a conscious effort to respond to them within a minute, it often took much longer than that.

All they wanted was to be heard, and in being heard to be understood, and in being understood to know that they were valued by me, and in being valued by me … to feel loved. In order to feel loved, they first needed to be heard.

How simple a thing it was and yet so powerful.

Gabriel and Grace are adults now, and I no longer enjoy the pleasant surprise of having a tiny hand quietly resting on my knee when I'm in the middle of a conversation.

I miss that.

THE LOVE@WORK ROADMAP

At the beginning of this chapter, I included an image of our roadmap for you to see all at once. I've divided our discussion on love at work into three main sections:

Part 1: Stepping from Darkness to Light

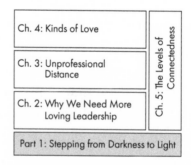

FIGURE 2:   PART 1 ROADMAP: STEPPING FROM DARKNESS TO LIGHT

There are four main questions I want to examine before we can have a transparent conversation about love at work. Part 1 addresses these questions.

Question 1: What is the impact of a lack of love in our workplaces?

Question 2: What is the relationship between love and professional distance?

Question 3: What is the definition of love in the workplace?

Question 4: What is the roadmap to take us from where we are to where we need to be?

Those questions correspond with chapters 2–5 of *Part 1: Stepping from Darkness to Light.*

In *Chapter 2: Death at Work*, we will tackle Question 1: What is the impact of a lack of love in our workplaces? We'll conduct a gap analysis to see where love has been systematically removed from our organisations, and we'll review some of the serious consequences that we have faced as a result.

In *Chapter 3: Unprofessional Distance*, we'll answer Question 2: What is the relationship between love and professional distance? We'll talk about the origin, definitions and misuses of the concept of professional distance. I'll also present a new paradigm for viewing as unprofessional so much of the distance we've created. And we'll try to close the gap.

In *Chapter 4: Kinds of Love*, we'll look at answering Question 3: What is the definition of love in the workplace? We'll look at what love means, and how ambiguity surrounding its definition has contributed to love's exclusion from our workplace vocabulary. I'll show you how love is defined in other languages, and we'll settle on a working definition and meaning for love at work.

In *Chapter 5: The Levels of Connectedness*, we'll answer Question 4: What is the roadmap to take us from where we are to where we need to be? We'll look at the five stages of human connectedness in brief. I'll introduce the process by which people move from feeling included to feeling loved, and I'll outline some principles that govern this process.

Part 2: Marching Towards Connectedness

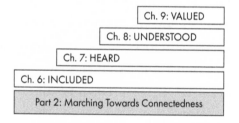

FIGURE 3:   PART 2 ROADMAP: MARCHING TOWARDS CONNECTEDNESS

There are five main steps governing the growth of human connectedness from basic inclusion to loving relationships. We'll discuss the first four stages in detail in Part 2, considering the effect of each stage on individuals and organisations. We'll look at some of the research that's been done at each stage and explore the bottom-line impact of helping our employees to feel included, heard, understood, and valued. And I'll give you practical tools for pursuing each stage of connectedness as a leader in your workplace context.

In *Chapter 6: Included*, we'll look at diversity, equity, and inclusion as the baseline for beginning the process towards a loving workplace. We'll also discuss psychological safety and the impact of social isolation.

In *Chapter 7: Heard*, we'll review the impact of employees feeling heard in an organisation. We'll explore how managers and leaders can invite more voices, and I'll provide practical tips for encouraging a workplace that allows employees to feel heard.

In *Chapter 8: Understood*, we'll examine the difference between feeling heard and feeling understood, and the importance of both. I'll also provide an overview of active listening stages and techniques for you to use.

In *Chapter 9: Valued*, we'll see how important it is that employees experience meaningful change in their workplace relationships, and I'll show you how care, curiosity, and learning contribute to your company's bottom line.

We won't be able to approach the final stage in the connectedness process until we deal with two more critical concerns about the application of love in the workplace: sex and romance, and attack and withdrawal.

Part 3: Running into Love at Work

| Ch. 12: Loving Leadership |
| Ch. 11: Kinds of Unlove |
| Ch. 10: Something to Talk About |
| **Part 3: Running into Love at Work** |

FIGURE 4:   PART 3 ROADMAP: RUNNING INTO LOVE AT WORK

In *Chapter 10: Something to Talk About* we'll address the challenges of sex and romance at work. We'll look at the growing phenomenon of work-spouses and review the critical conversation surrounding workplace sexual harassment. We'll clarify the boundaries for love at work and clear up some common misconceptions about sex and romance in companies.

In *Chapter 11: Kinds of Unlove,* we'll look at attack and withdrawal as types of unlove in the workplace. I'll also give you some input on exclusionary behaviour and prescribe reconciliation as an appropriate response.

In *Chapter 12: Loving Leadership,* we'll review other leadership writers' attempts to address love in the workplace. We'll see the impact of loving leadership on workplace culture, and we'll finally have a clear picture of what love in the workplace should look like. I'll also share the qualities of a loving leader, and how you can express love at work in specific ways.

WELCOME TO THE JOURNEY

I can't relate well enough in words how excited I am that you're on this journey with me. I don't want to give you the impression that I have all of the answers or that I've tackled every challenge we'll face along the way. I'd like you to think of me more as a guide than guru, as we explore this relatively uncharted territory together. I hope you'll agree with me that as challenging as this conversation will be at times, it's worthwhile and even long overdue.

Darkness only exists where light is absent. All the light needs to do is shine, and the darkness has no choice but to run away. But in order to appreciate the light that *Love@Work* can produce for us, we must first peer into the darkness it is intended to dispel. That's what we'll do in *Part 1: Stepping from Darkness to Light*.

PART ONE

STEPPING FROM DARKNESS TO LIGHT

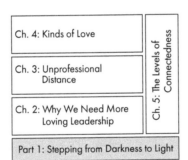

REMY'S RESIGNATION

CHAPTER 2

DEATH AT WORK

Why We Need More Loving Leadership

"LOVE IS AN UNTAMED FORCE. WHEN WE TRY TO CON-TROL IT, IT DESTROYS US. WHEN WE TRY TO IMPRISON IT, IT ENSLAVES US. WHEN WE TRY TO UNDERSTAND IT, IT LEAVES US LOST AND CONFUSED."

—PAULO COELHO

REMY'S RESIGNATION

It was an average Tuesday morning when siblings Noémie, Raphaël, Juliette, and Matthieu said goodbye to their father as he left for work. Remy Louvradoux wished his kids a good day at school, kissed his wife Hélène, jumped in the car, and pulled into the office parking lot at about 7 am. He had started working at France Télécom when he was 20 years old, almost four decades ago. He'd worked hard and rose through the ranks to become an executive.

But at the age of 57, Remy had found himself relegated to a mid-level role as a Prevention Officer. His new job was to help the company to identify and prevent mental health crises at the Mérignac branch near Bordeaux. It seemed like a good thing to do, but he quickly learned that France Télécom CEO, Didier Lombard, had no intention of helping his employees.

Remy's new office was windowless, contained no computer and no phone. So, he wrote letters, not only about those who were suffering, but about his own conditions. None of his letters was answered. It may have seemed obvious that Remy should resign, but it wasn't that easy.

He was too old to be hired at his income level in another company, and yet he felt that there was nothing he could do to appease his leaders under their new policies. And there was nothing he could do to add value to the employees he tried desperately to serve. He was stuck.

> **HE HAD INVESTED NO LESS THAN 100,000 HOURS OF HIS OWN LIFE IN THAT ECONOMIC COMMUNITY. HOURS, DAYS, MONTHS, AND YEARS THAT HE WOULD NEVER GET BACK.**

He had been 37 years in his company. It was all he knew. He spent more time each day with his teammates and colleagues than with his wife and kids. It wasn't just a job for Remy, it was more than half of his life. He had invested no less than 100,000 hours in that economic community. Hours, days, months, and years that he would never get back – time that seemed to be worth less to his bosses with each day that passed.

The job wasn't all of him, but it sure was a lot of him. So, when he arrived at work that day, stuck between a future of isolation torture in a windowless room or irrelevance on the streets outside, he accepted that he had finally burnt out.

Full of despair, anger, and hopelessness, Remy Louvradoux set himself on fire in the parking lot of France Telecom on April 26th, 2011, killing himself just days before Noémie's 18th birthday.[3]

He was not alone. The unions reported more than 60 suicides due to work-related stress among France Télécom employees between 2006 and 2010; there were an additional 12 attempted suicides in that time and 8 cases of clinical depression that we're aware of (presumably many more remained unreported).[4]

In 2009, 49-year-old Yonnel Dervin stabbed himself in the office after being demoted, and a 51-year-old employee cited "overwork" and "management by terror" as the conditions

3   Bollendorf, S. (2013). *Le grand incendie*. Retrieved from http://www.samuel-bollendorff.com/fr/le-grand-incendie-2/; 35 employees kill themselves. Will their bosses go to jail? (2019). *The Business Times*. https://www.businesstimes.com.sg/startups-tech/technology/35-employees-kill-themselves-will-their-bosses-go-jail.

4   Suicides à France Télécom: Pourquoi la prevention n'a pas fonctionné. (2016). *Alternatives Economiques*. Retrieved from https://www.alternatives-economiques.fr/suicides-a-france-telecom-prevention-na-fonctionne/00012327; Waters, S. (2019). Suicide as Corporate Murder: France Télécom on Trial. *Truthout*. Retrieved from https://truthout.org/articles/suicide-as-corporate-murder-france-telecom-on-trial/.

leading to his final words: "I am killing myself because of my job at France Télécom. That's the only reason."

How could this happen?

The company had been struggling financially, and growing pressure to reduce expenses and increase productivity were the underlying conditions that led to a workplace culture of fear and stress. To try and remove more than 22,000 employees, Didier Lombard had launched a crusade of marginalisation against employees he wanted out. He made their lives so miserable that one journalist noted, "At France Télécom, worker suicides were not an aberration of the system, but the deliberate outcome."[5]

Remy's passing was both ironic and tragic, as it was supposed to be his job to prevent such events. Instead, in his own suicide note addressed to the CEO, he acknowledged that he felt he had no choice but to join those he was asked to serve, not as a leader with a solution, but as one of those employees who saw suicide as the only possible solution. He wrote:[6]

---

5   Waters, S. (2019). Suicide as Corporate Murder: France Télécom on Trial. *Truthout*. Retrieved from https://truthout.org/articles/suicide-as-corporate -murder-france-telecom-on-trial/.

6   Bollendorf, S. (2013). *Le grand incendie*. Retrieved from http://www.sam-uel-bollendorff.com/fr/le-grand-incendie-2/; 35 employees kill them-selves. Will their bosses go to jail? (2019). *The Business Times*. https:// www.businesstimes.com.sg/startups-tech/technology/35-employees-kill-themselves-will-their-bosses-go-jail, translation and paraphrasing mine.

Mr CEO,

I would like to react to the wave of suicides which the company is currently facing. What is the population affected by these suicides? Civil servants over the age of 50 with forced reassignment. I'm in that segment, and I am one too many.

I'll introduce myself quickly: working primarily and purely to earn a living in a positive service environment. Harassment suffered from my direct line manager. Stuck at a lower managerial level. Put in the trash.

My observation: there are people in high-risk situations, they no longer expect any support, they no longer expect anything.

My fears: this situation is endemic because nothing is done to deal with it. Suicide remains THE SOLUTION.

It's sad, but who benefits from this crime?

R. L.
Preventer in the Human Resources Department

Remy's letter to his CEO gives us a clear view of the kind of actions that unloving leaders are capable of inspiring in their employees. Love in leadership matters; for Remy it was a matter of life and death.

During the decade-long court trial that followed, Remy's daughter Noémie testified that her father's suicide was the inevitable outcome of Lombard's strategy. She stated, "They murdered my father and my family life. They robbed us of our lives…. My father's death was the fulfilment of their objective."[7]

In 2019, the French courts found seven executives guilty of employee harassment, sentencing the former CEO to a year in prison, and fining the company 75,000 Euros. This was the punishment for leading a workplace culture in which employee suicides averaged one a month, for five straight years.

And that was just one company.

Take a deep breath. As leaders, we need to peer into the darkness to understand how badly we need the light.

LOVELESSNESS IS KILLING US

I wish I could tell you that France Télécom was an anomaly, but it's not. In recent years, a number of cruise line employees have committed suicide citing their working conditions.[8] Then there's that string of employee suicides at Renault under the leadership of CEO Carlos Ghosn between 2009 and 2011.[9] Oh,

---

7   Waters, S. (2019). Suicide as Corporate Murder: France Télécom on Trial. *Truthout*. Retrieved from https://truthout.org/articles/suicide-as-corporate-murder-france-telecom-on-trial/.

8   Carr, Austin. (2020). The cruise ship suicides. *Bloomberg*. Retrieved from https://www.bloomberg.com/features/2020-cruise-ship-suicides/.

9   Diem, W. (2009). Unions blame work pressure for suicides at Renault. Retrieved from https://www.wardsauto.com/news-analysis/unions-blame-work-pressure-suicides-renault.

and don't forget that fourteen employees committed suicide by leaping from the factory windows at Foxconn in 2010 under CEO Terry Gou.[10] The suicide nets that were subsequently installed at their factories are still there.

The news isn't better in the United States, where suicide rates among American workers rose steadily between 1999 and 2018 before beginning to decline between 2018 and 2020.[11] People at the highest risk for work related suicide are "military members, medical professionals, police officers, veterans, farmers, fire fighters, and blue-collar workers."[12] A single suicide affects an average of 135 of people, with co-workers commonly suffering from decreased performance and feelings of grief and guilt.[13]

There are lots of workplace conditions that can lead employees to that depth of despair, for example:

1. *Environmental*: occupational dangers, hard physical labour, and poor ergonomics;

---

10   Merchant, Brian. (2017). *The one device: the secret history of the iPhone*. Little, Brown and Company.

11   Hedegaard, H., & Warner, M. (2021). Suicide mortality in the United States, 1999-2019; Garnett, M. F., Curtin, S. C., & Stone, D. M. (2022). Suicide mortality in the United States, 2000-2020.

12   Howard, M. C., Follmer, K. B., Smith, M. B., Tucker, R. P., & Van Zandt, E. C. (2022). Work and suicide: An interdisciplinary systematic literature review. *Journal of Organisational Behaviour, 43*(2), 260-285 (p. 266).

13   DeRanieri, J. T., Clements, P. T., & Henry, G. C. (2002). When catastrophe happens: Assessment and intervention after sudden traumatic death. *Journal of Psychosocial Nursing, 40*(4), 30-37.; Mericle, B. P. (1993). When a colleague commits suicide. *Journal of Psychosocial Nursing, 31*(9), 11-13.

2. *Social*: exclusion, mistreatment, and burdensomeness;
3. *Hope-Based*: lack of transferable skills, lack of a career plan, or disruptive technology;
4. *Other*: substance abuse, mental illness, membership in a marginalised social group;[14] and
5. *Involuntary Job Loss*: redundancies or layoffs.[15]

At its worst, an unloving workplace can lead to employee suicide, but suicide isn't the only mortality risk for stressed-out employees. Employees who have low job control (meaning they don't have much say in what they do, how they do it, or for how long) have a 21% increased risk of dying overall, and are 50% more likely to die of heart disease than the average person.[16]

But perhaps the most unloving thing we can do in our organisations is to remove people from them. Humans are social animals, and our survival throughout history has been based on belonging to tribes that will provide for us and protect us (**FP2.1**). Businesses are just modern forms of economic tribes, from a group psychology perspective. And although firing people for reasons that have nothing to do with their job performance

---

14   Howard, M. C., Follmer, K. B., Smith, M. B., Tucker, R. P., & Van Zandt, E. C. (2022). Work and suicide: An interdisciplinary systematic literature review. Journal of Organisational Behaviour, 43(2), 260-285 (p. 266).

15   Garcy, A. M., & Vågerö, D. (2013). Unemployment and suicide during and after a deep recession: A longitudinal study of 3.4 million Swedish men and women. *American Journal of Public Health, 103*(6), 1031-1038.

16   Taouk, Y., Spittal, M. J., LaMontagne, A. D., & Milner, A. J. (2020). Psychosocial work stressors and risk of all-cause and coronary heart disease mortality. *Scandinavian Journal of Work, Environment & Health, 46*(1), 19-31.

> **HUMANS ARE SOCIAL ANIMALS, AND OUR SURVIVAL THROUGHOUT HISTORY HAS BEEN BASED ON BELONGING TO TRIBES THAT WILL PROVIDE FOR US AND PROTECT US. BUSINESSES ARE JUST MODERN FORMS OF ECONOMIC TRIBES, FROM A GROUP PSYCHOLOGY PERSPECTIVE.**

is a commonly accepted management strategy, it's unloving, unnatural, and it has a devastating impact both on the employees who are let go, and what remains of the company culture (**FP2.2**).

Layoffs are connected to significant declines in both mental and physical health, even when adjusted for pre-existing causes of both.[17] The most frequently reported side-effect of redundancies is depression,[18] especially in the case of older employees whose spouses may also suffer depression as a result of their being let go.[19] This is such a big issue in the social sciences

17 Burgard, S. A., Brand, J. E., & House, J. S. (2007). Toward a better estimation of the effect of job loss on health. *Journal of Health and Social Behaviour 2007, 48*(December), 369-384; Janske H. W. Eersel, Toon W. Taris & Paul A. Boelen (2020) Reciprocal relations between symptoms of complicated grief, depression, and anxiety following job loss: A cross-lagged analysis. *Clinical Psychologist, 24*(3), 276-284.

18 Kasl, S., & Jones, B. (2000). The impact of job loss and retirement on health. In L. F. Berkman & I. Kawachi (Eds.), *Social epidemiology*. Oxford University Press; van Eersel, J. H. W., Taris, T. W. & Boelen, P. A. (2020). Complicated grief following job loss: Risk factors for its development and maintenance. *Scandinavian Journal of Psychology, 61*, 698-706.

19 Siegel, M., H., Bradley, E., Gallo, W., & V Kasl, S. (2003). Impact of husbands' involuntary job loss on wives' mental health, among older adults. *The Journals of Gerontology, Series B, Psychological Sciences and Social Sciences*.

that the *Journal of Managerial Psychology* once dedicated a whole issue to the psychological effects of job loss.[20]

Several studies found that an employee's risk of death increases by up to 60% after being made redundant, even when you correct for pre-existing mental conditions and addictions.[21] These employees end up dying of heart attack, stroke,[22] or suicide[23] around the time of being let go from their jobs (**FP2.3**).

This is a matter of life and death.

The cold truth is that whether employees are marginalised and devalued within their jobs, or cut out from their economic communities involuntarily, some of them will die as a result (directly or indirectly) of those managerial decisions. That's the science of it. And it should make every CEO shudder.

---

20   Karren, R. (2012). Introduction to the special issue on job loss. *Journal of Managerial Psychology, 27*(8), 772-779.

21   Noelke, C., & Beckfield, J. (2014). Recessions, job loss, and mortality among older US adults. *American Journal of Public Health, 104*(11), 126-134.

22   Gallo, W. T., Bradley, E. H., & Falba, T. A. (2004). Involuntary job loss as a risk factor for subsequent myocardial infarction and stroke: Findings from the Health and Retirement Survey. *American Journal of Industrial Medicine, 45*(5), 408–416.; Gallo, W. T., Teng, H.-M., Falba, T. A., Kasl, S. V., Bradley, E. H., & Krumholz, H. M. (2006). The impact of late career job loss on myocardial infarction and stroke: A 10-year follow up using the Health and Retirement Survey. *Journal of Occupational Environmental Medicine, 63*(10), 683-687.

23   Garcy, A. M., & Vågerö, D. (2013). Unemployment and suicide during and after a deep recession: A longitudinal study of 3.4 million Swedish men and women. *American Journal of Public Health 103*(6), 1031-1038.

Those deaths, including the suicide of Remy Louvradoux, are the statistical outcome of management and leadership strategies that allow or pursue social violence against employees in either of the two extremes of unlove: attack (ostracism within the workplace) and withdrawal (involuntary job loss).

These extreme strategies, and the extreme results they lead to, are not the most common expressions of an unloving workplace. They may be the most dramatic, but our employees often experience dehumanisation and unlove in more subtle ways, long before the stress registers as either attack or withdrawal.

DEHUMANISATION OF EMPLOYEES AND THE IMPACT ON MENTAL HEALTH

Half of the American workforce is stressed at work, and a quarter of all employees in the United States report that work is their single greatest source of stress. More specifically, employees who are reminded that "time is money" are more stressed at work. Other contributing factors include low social support, increases

> MANAGEMENT IDEAS SUCH AS HUMAN-AS-RESOURCE, TIME-AS-MONEY, SHAREHOLDER SUPREMACY, AND PROFESSIONAL DISTANCE, ARE ALL THOUGHT TO IMPROVE BUSINESS EFFICIENCY. BUT IT'S NOT TRUE.

in expectations of work productivity, and a bad relationship with their line manager (**FP2.4**).[24]

Management ideas such as human-as-resource, time-as-money, shareholder supremacy, and professional distance, are all thought to improve business efficiency. They don't. These are the lies of cold economists and bad consultants. I learned some of them when studying for my MBA! These management practices, which come at the cost of social connection and the mental health of employees, actually end up creating more inefficiencies (**FP2.5**).

> Workers from all socioeconomic backgrounds are being controlled to an increasingly sophisticated extent in order to maximise the amount of work it is possible to extract from a human being. Most of these workers are experiencing a high level of stress as a result, and very few are receiving any significant financial benefit from their increased efficiency. Even those who [do] … suffer from a lack of family and leisure time and the accompanying social and psychological problems.[25]

Even before the 2020 pandemic, reports were circulating that 60% of workers in the United Kingdom experience workplace

---

24 Pfeffer, J., & Carney, D. R. (2018). The economic evaluation of time can cause stress. *Academy of Management Discoveries*, 4(1), 74-93.

25 Blakeley, K., & Blakeley, C. (2021). *Leading with love: Rehumanising the workplace*. Routledge, (p. 4).

conditions that decrease mental health.[26] Post-pandemic studies have found that 71% of employees in the United States strongly agreed that their mental health was being negatively affected by their workplace; 23% said they didn't care at all about what happened to their colleagues or clients.[27]

Seriously? Every fourth person doesn't care at all about the people they work with? That's horrible. Maybe that's why there's been a 19% rise in workplace bullying over the decade up to 2019.[28]

A survey by JobSage (2023) found that 41% of Americans considered quitting their jobs due to mental health concerns. They cite the leading causes of workplace stress as compensation (42%) and overwork (39%). Burnout is on the rise, yet half of employees say that their company doesn't do enough to support their mental health. Half of employees have taken a "mental health day," while half of *those* didn't even tell anyone it *was* a mental health day. In fact, 1 in 4 employees won't even talk about mental health at work (**FP2.6**).[29]

---

26   Parsonage, M., & Saini, G. (2017). Mental health at work. *Center for Mental Health.*

27   Adams, T., Reinert, M., Fritze, D., & Nguyen, T. (2021). *Mind the workplace: Work health survey 2021.*

28   Robinson, B. (2019) New study says workplace bullying on the rise: What you can do during National Bullying Prevention Month. *Forbes.* Retrieved from https://www.forbes.com/sites/bryanrobinson/2019/10/11/new-study-says-workplace-bullying-on-rise-what-can-you-do-during-national-bullying-prevention-month/?sh=821fdb32a0d4.

29   Duncan, K. (2023). Survey: Compensation is the top factor of work-related stress in 2023. *JobSage.* Retrieved from https://www.jobsage.com/blog/survey-employees-mental-health-in-2023/.

And what is this workplace mental health crisis costing our organisations? Can you imagine? I can. For now, let's just agree that the lack of love at work is something everyone should be paying attention to. Something needs to be done, and we're the leaders. We're responsible.

STARTING FROM LOVE

We need a starting place for addressing the negative conditions and effects of workplace stress, social disconnection, and mental health issues – and their impact on performance and profitability (and life expectancy). I think that starting place should be the most inclusive, connected, and healthy human condition we can possibly imagine: love. I think we should respond to the darkness with the brightest light we have.

To do this though, let's pull back from the devastating outcomes of suicide and heart attacks to look even more closely at the gap created between employees in organisations. Rather than lingering on generic causes of workplace stress, I'd like us to focus on of the most subtle and challenging root causes of disconnection between people in the workplace. I want to study the gap created by professional distance to see if love can help to fill it. As leaders, we should be building cultures that encourage people to connect as much as they can (rather than avoid the connections we all need). Then, perhaps, we can find our way towards a more loving organisational culture.

FIRST PRINCIPLES

FP2.1 Humans are social animals. We need to belong to groups of people in order to survive.

FP2.2 Companies are modern forms of economic tribes.

FP2.3 Being made redundant can be fatal.

FP2.4 Workplace culture and environment have significant impacts on employee mental health.

FP2.5 What the consultant says is good for profit might be bad for people.

FP2.6 Workplace stress is on the rise, with compensation and overwork being the leading causes.

NEXT STEPS

1. Recognise the importance of the workplace on your employees' quality of life.
2. Don't fire anyone who doesn't deserve it.
3. Don't manipulate people into quitting when they have nowhere else to go.
4. Invest in your employees' mental health and wellbeing.

RANDY AND ROSALIE

CHAPTER 3

UNPROFESSIONAL DISTANCE

How Can We Bridge This Artificially
Manufactured Space between Us?

"THE PRICE OF GREATNESS IS RESPONSIBILITY."

—WINSTON CHURCHILL

KISS, BOW, OR SHAKE HANDS

I stepped into the boardroom in Abu Dhabi, removed my suit jacket, and took my seat on the opposite side of the table from the door. One by one, with big smiles on their faces, came in to greet me. I knew everyone, because they had each attended one of my training programs or been coached by me directly.

- Sarah was a Tunisian woman in her mid-twenties who wore a hijab covering her hair. She reached her arms out to me and gave me a big welcoming hug.
- Stella was from the UK, a thirty-something married woman with the brightest smile you've ever seen. She shook my hand and took her seat.

- Mariam was a single Emirati woman in her early forties who wore a hijab as well. I did not extend my hand to shake hers, but I was welcomed by her with another amazing smile and a genuine expression of joy that we were seeing each other again.
- Mahad was a UK-born Pakistani man in his mid-forties. I shook his hand and pulled him in for a big hug before the five of us sat down to discuss a coaching programme for the executives in their company.

I got as close to each of them as I could have in that environment, physically and emotionally, and I would consider all of them not just as colleagues but as friends. And I should add that their individual cultural expressions of appropriate contact are neither morally good nor bad, they're just cultural. But how did I know whom to hug, shake hands with, or avoid touching altogether? How did I know what they would each consider to be appropriate contact?

And why couldn't they all just hug me, which is what I actually wanted? Well the answer lies in understanding and respecting the cultural and social practices of our colleagues and clients. In order to know how to treat someone, we need to know them personally.

HOW IS THE HEALTH OF YOUR FAMILY?

It was even more complicated when I lived in Yemen. Although I haven't seen him in more than twelve years, Khalid still writes to me every few months to see how I am and ask about my family. We worked closely together when I lived in Taiz, and I often chewed qat with him in his house. He spoke perfect English and was educated in Germany. He knew the Western world very well, but we didn't live in the Western world.

In the five years that I worked with Khalid, and over the thousands of hours that we sat together at his place, I only ever met his wife Yasmeen once. She was standing at a comfortable three-metre distance, with her face fully covered. That was only after two years of knowing Khalid, and it never happened again.

Yasmeen and my first wife Dawn were close friends, too, and in any other country the four of us would likely have been seen sharing dinner together or taking our kids to the park as families. When we'd return home after visiting them (in gender-segregated living rooms), Dawn and I would swap our two versions of the same stories. In this way, we could feel we'd connected with our friends' spouses as well. After a few years I felt like I knew Yasmeen, so it was worrying for me to hear from Dawn one day that Yasmeen had been rushed to the hospital in serious condition.

I wanted to support Yasmeen and I wanted to be a good friend to Khalid. But I knew better than to call him and ask about his wife. In Yemeni culture, a man should never enquire about another man's wife. To do so means that she has been occupying your thoughts, and that's a breach of professional distance.

I WANTED TO SUPPORT YASMEEN AND I WANTED TO BE A GOOD FRIEND TO KHALID. BUT I KNEW BETTER THAN TO CALL HIM AND ASK ABOUT HIS WIFE.

So, I called Khalid and asked him, "How is the health of your family?" Because that's the right way to enquire. To which he replied, "We have some struggles, but we are getting what we need." His use of the royal "we" meant that he could honour my concern without accusing me of having given any thought to his wife.

Yasmeen recovered in time, but I called Khalid every day for a couple of weeks just to check in. He was grateful that I had honoured him and his wife through our elaborate social game, and he knew that my concern was genuine, and as much to do with my own wife's friendship with Yasmeen as my friendship with Khalid.

I know this might be a confronting scene for some Western leaders to read about, but I don't want you to get wrong impression here. Khalid loves Yasmeen, truly. I knew that from Dawn. And Yasmeen never once would have described her culture as oppressive or restrictive, or herself as an "object" in her culture.

That's just the way the world works in Yemen. It's not moral, it's cultural.[30] For five years I worked and socialised with Yemeni men – and never asked about, met, or otherwise even acknowledged in conversation, any of their wives. It would have been unprofessional if I had.

TO LOVE, OR NOT TO LOVE

As the world has become more integrated and globalised, we are spending more time with people whose social norms are not like our own, and we need to figure out what kinds of intimacies are appropriate and not appropriate in the workplace. Living and working in Yemen, and now in Dubai, has on occasion presented challenges for a Canadian-born hugger like me. I have on more than one occasion extended my hand instinctively to an Emirati woman, who will then politely maintain eye contact with me and not reciprocate the gesture. Yikes.

Yet I also have experienced incredible intimacy with colleagues and business contacts. Mahed, from the boardroom above, is a

---

30 One of my Swedish friends helped me to see that this story might be challenging for some readers. It was interesting to me, living and working in Yemen, that what we Westerners considered as the objectification of women in Yemen (the hijab, gender segregation, etc.) was considered freedom by most of the women living there. To the women of Yemen, they could be judged on their merits, not their looks. And they viewed some of our Western values (e.g. legal pornography and sex-driven media and advertising) as objectifying of women. Having spent 16 years in the Arabian Peninsula, I'm of the opinion that each woman should decide for herself whether she feels objectified in her culture.

very close friend of mine. I stay in his home whenever I am in Abu Dhabi, we share meals together, and we tell each other things that would be considered secrets (and definitely not discussed in a business setting). I would say without hesitation that I love Mahed in the traditional sense: as a brother, a confidant, and a close friend. Just as I love Khalid. But, with a regret that led to me writing this book, I've never told either of them that I love them.

I've never said, "Khalid, I love you," even though it's true.

Why not? What's so hard about that?

PROFESSIONAL DISTANCE

Any good love at work strategy should start with a gap analysis. If love is the solution, there must be a problem that it addresses, right? In the last chapter we looked at the darkest consequences of unlove in the workplace, but now I want to look at something a lot more subtle. You might not think of love as unprofessional *per se*, but love is certainly opposed to the manufacturing of distance in human relationships – and professional distance is exactly that: manufactured.

So is professional distance a kind of unlove at work?

Let's look at where this gap originated, and what makes distance between humans "professional."

Most companies now have some kind of policy describing expectations for employee conduct. Essentially guidelines on professional distance, they include warnings that employees should avoid behaviours that might be perceived as inappropriate. They include:

- Providing special favours or privileges to colleagues;
- Physical contact that exceeds a handshake or a brief pat on the back;
- Using offensive or inappropriate language;
- Making sexually suggestive or offensive jokes or comments;
- Sending inappropriate or offensive messages;
- Invading personal space;
- Engaging in romantic or sexual relationships with colleagues;
- Offering or accepting gifts that are perceived as inappropriate or extravagant.

I've seen these and more in a number of employee handbooks. I'm not saying we should allow people to use offensive language (for example). In fact, I tend to agree with all of the principles above, but they do seem rather undefined and subjective. For instance, who defines what an "inappropriate" message is? And who decides whether a pat on the back was sufficiently "brief?" The Chief Human Resources Officer (CHRO)? The colleague whose back has been patted? A committee of back-patting specialists brought in to advise the legal team on the liability risks of back patting? Who defines the distance as "professional"?

Different companies and different cultures have very different definitions of professional distance as well. Some of them are cause for concern:

- In France it is often expected to greet female co-workers with a kiss on the cheek.[31]
- In the US some companies have "love contracts" that require romantically involved co-workers to declare the mutual consent of their workplace relationships and release the company of any liability stemming from a breakup.[32]
- Employees in Japanese companies have reported being required to greet their "special" female colleagues, and to greet their bosses' dog.[33]
- A lawyer at American Express cautions that appropriate hugging is at shoulder level, infrequent, brief, and silent (i.e. no making comments or whispering during the hug).[34]

---

31   Snippets of Paris. (2023). French work culture: 19 differences that will astonish. *Ansi Hardi SAS.* Retrieved from https://snippetsofparis.com/french-work-culture/.

32   Wilkie, D. (2013). Forbidden love: Workplace-romance policies now stricter. *SHRM.* Retrieved from https://www.shrm.org/resourcesand-tools/hr-topics/employee-relations/pages/forbidden-love-workplace-romance-policies-stricter.aspx.

33   Employees reveal absurd company regulations. (2011). *Japan Today.* Retrieved from https://japantoday.com/category/features/kuchikomi/employees-reveal-absurd-company-regulations.

34   Nicolas, L. (2020). Will HR need a hugging policy when employees return to the office? *Unleash.* Retrieved from https://www.unleash.ai/covid-19/when-can-we-hug-again/.

- Netflix has banned its staff from maintaining eye contact for more than five seconds.[35]

In the wake of the firing of the *Today* show host Matt Lauer from NBC, the company's policies were amended to restrict hugging: "If you wish to hug a colleague, you have to do a quick hug, then an immediate release, and step away to avoid body contact."[36] Furthermore, any employee who witnesses a potential breach of the hugging policy is required to report it, on threat of termination if they don't.

Does that sound like a warm and welcoming working environment to you? Would you feel psychologically safe in a company that's measuring the duration of your eye contact and requires your colleagues to judge and report the "quickness" of your hugs? Are we perhaps overcorrecting a bit with a legislative approach to relationship building? Professional distance, though meant to facilitate multicultural collaboration, can inadvertently create barriers when generalised (**FP3.1**).

Please don't get me wrong here. I agree that people should be working in environments where they feel safe and supported,

---

35   Hooton, C. (2018). Netflix film crews "banned from looking at each other for longer than five seconds" in #metoo crackdown. *Independent*. Retrieved from https://www.independent.co.uk/arts-entertainment/tv/news/netflix-sexual-harassment-training-rules-me-too-flirting-on-set-a8396431.html.

36   Smith, E. (2017). NBC orders staff to rat out misbehaving colleagues or be fired. Retrieved from https://pagesix.com/2017/12/25/nbc-tightens-sexual-harassment-rules-following-matt-lauer-mess/.

but I don't think we should be delegating the responsibility for defining those environments to our corporate legal teams. I don't think we're heading in the right direction here.

Neuroendocrinologist (brain guru) Robert Sapolsky (2017) notes that professional distance is an impossible problem to solve, since it's completely subjective. One person can feel a pat on the back as sexual, and another can be hugged tightly and experience only empathy.[37] In any case, this is definitely a concern for us huggers. It feels unnatural to me that I should be told that back patting is risky behaviour in a community of people where I'm planning to spend half of my life every day. I think there might be a better way for us to approach the problem of professional distance.

> IT FEELS UNNATURAL TO ME THAT I SHOULD BE TOLD THAT BACK PATTING IS RISKY BEHAVIOUR IN A COMMUNITY OF PEOPLE WHERE I'M PLANNING TO SPEND HALF OF MY LIFE EVERY DAY.

The formal concept of professional distance started in the field of psychology. Therapists needed a way to describe the emotional, mental, and physical boundaries that would help them to remain objective while serving clients with emotional trauma and pain. Humans are naturally empathetic, so it's difficult to help people who are hurting all day without feeling

---

37   Sapolsky, R. M. (2017). Behave: The biology of humans at our best and worst.

a bit injured yourself. Professional distance was created to help. The idea moved quickly into the medical profession, to keep doctors from becoming too emotionally invested in their patients. I agree that professional distance for therapists and doctors still makes a lot of sense, but it's a lot less clear to me in the business context.

RANDY AND ROSALIE

Randy was twenty years old when he got a job in the accounting pool at a consulting firm. He enjoyed working with numbers, and he was good at his job. He got along well with his colleagues and those in different departments he regularly interacted with. It wasn't long before he was a valued member of the team. This wasn't surprising, since one of the core values of the company was "family"; it described the kind of social environment they wanted to foster.

Soon, Randy became closer with his work colleagues than with his parents and siblings. This was especially true of his boss, Rosalie, whom he saw as kind of a second mother to him. She made him feel accepted and cared for in his new city. Within a few months, most of his friends were from among his newly adopted tribe of workmates.

During this time of entering the workforce, making friends, and figuring out his place in society, Randy was also trying to come to terms with his sexual identity. Having been raised in a conservative Christian home, he had struggled for a long time to understand his attraction to men. He didn't want to tell his parents, but he needed someone to talk to.

Rosalie accepted the meeting request immediately, not knowing what it was about. But it wasn't long before Randy quietly shared with her his emerging awareness of his homosexuality and asked her for advice. "What should I do?" he said to an empathetic and principles-driven Rosalie.

I'm going to hit pause here.

Before I tell you what advice Rosalie gave to Randy, I want to highlight a few things:

1. The nature of the conversation they were having was intimate.
2. They were having that conversation in their workplace.
3. The "family" value of the company helped create the kind of trust necessary to provide psychological safety for Randy to say something.
4. Randy's sense of belonging and care with Rosalie was necessary for him to have chosen her for this (potentially) breakthrough conversation. And,
5. Randy's homosexuality was not a choice he was making, but a discovery about himself.

Those are all good things, right? Those are things we want in our organisations, don't we? Don't we want people to "find themselves" in our workplaces and feel supported in doing so?

These were the environmental factors that led to Randy and Rosalie's equally appropriate and inappropriate conversation. Clearly Randy was not observing professional distance here, and he was expecting the same from Rosalie. He might not have been in direct breach of any of the inappropriate behaviours listed in the employee handbook, but this was well outside of a work-related discussion. And yet there he was, a young man in his boss' office, with his heart on the table.

Now, how should Rosalie respond? Remember that the company had intentionally pursued the environmental and affective culture elements leading to this conversation, and had done so while empowering an emotionally intelligent leader like Rosalie. Rosalie cares about Randy, but it's important to know that her personal beliefs are like those of Randy's parents. Rosalie believes that homosexuality is not natural. So what should she say?

> *Possibility 1, too much professional distance*: Rosalie asks Randy to leave her office because she doesn't want to discuss the subject with him. Randy feels dejected and confused.

> *Possibility 2, too little professional distance*: Rosalie tells Randy that the Bible as she understands it is against homosexuality, and he should resist his "sinful desires." Randy again feels dejected and confused.

Rosalie's being of the same school of thought as Randy's parents might be partly why the two got along so well, why Randy thinks of Rosalie as a kind of mother figure.

But professional distance is necessary in order to protect Randy's autonomy. He needs to be able to make his own choices, and that means Rosalie can't bring her value judgement into the conversation.

So what did she actually do?

> AT ITS BEST, PROFESSIONAL DISTANCE PROTECTS THE OTHER PERSON FROM BEING CONFRONTED BY YOUR DIFFERING VALUES.

Rosalie politely listened to Randy and withheld her own judgement. She didn't give Randy advice but thanked him for confiding in her and expressed gratitude that they had the kind of relationship where he felt safe to talk to her about personal things. Randy would need to make his own choices, but he certainly felt a lot better just getting that secret out with someone he trusted and admired.

Professional distance requires employers and colleagues to withhold their own value judgements in an interpersonal relationship. This is done out of respect for employee autonomy. At its best, professional distance protects the other person from being confronted by your differing values (**FP3.2**).

I wanted to hug Mariam.

I wanted to ask Khalid how his wife was feeling.

I still want to tell Mahed that I love him.

I respected Mariam's autonomy by choosing a kind of greeting that was appropriate for her. I respected Khalid's autonomy when choosing how to indirectly ask about his wife. I respect Mahed's culture in withholding the word "love" from my description of our friendship. But let's face it, this is a book about love at work, so maybe I need to expose myself to some risk in the interest of modelling good leadership.

So here we go …

I know for a fact that Mahed (not his real name) will read this book. You know who you are, Mahed, so here it is, for the record: I love you, brother. Truly. I'm so glad to know you and your family. You're an incredible leader both in and out of the office, and you add value to my life every time we meet.

Right, back to the subject …

PROPER DISTANCE

Now that we know professional distance is designed to protect others from our own values, let's see if we can find a path towards a more loving work environment by examining that idea. For example, what if they don't want to be protected from your values? What if they value your values, even if your values are different from theirs?

Historically, we really didn't have to protect people from our values very much. Consider that only a century ago, prior to air travel, most humans spent most of their lives in the same place they were born. They did the same work their father or mother did, followed the same religion as most of their neighbours, and heard the same stories as their ancestors, co-workers, and friends.

Interacting with people whose values were very different was also very rare. People didn't have to manufacture professional distance, because there was no real need for it. Everyone had shared values, so they all knew whether to hug or shake hands.

The industrial revolution changed that completely. Suddenly people weren't stuck in their tribes or cities anymore. They didn't have to rely on their father or mother to define their place in society. You could be a productive member of society outside of your city, tribe, and religion. With the invention of factories, and innovations in transportation, anyone from anywhere could travel to work in any place, so long as they had a skill to offer to their new economic tribe (their company).

But mixing the world up like that means that you are much more likely to work alongside people who are not like you. They aren't necessarily from your tribe, city, or religion. Their values are probably different from yours, and you need a way to make sure that your differing values don't get in the way of working together.

> PROFESSIONAL DISTANCE WAS MANUFACTURED RIGHT ALONGSIDE THE STEAM ENGINE AND THE ASSEMBLY LINE, SO THAT OUR PERSONAL VALUES DON'T GET IN THE WAY OF OUR COLLECTIVE INTEREST IN OUR NEW ECONOMIC TRIBES.

Professional distance was manufactured right alongside the steam engine and the assembly line, so that our personal values don't get in the way of our collective interest in our new economic tribes. In his 1997 review of the concept, Mike Martin defines professional distance as:

> Selectively withholding expression of everyday values in professional life, whether the values are embodied in emotions, preferences, relationships, conduct, or ideals … Withholding expression of personal values might imply avoiding particular actions, habits, intimate relationships, emotions, biases, or ordinary moral reasons.[38]

---

38 Martin, M. W. (1997). Professional distance. *International Journal of Applied Philosophy 11*(2) 39-50.

He goes on to say that there is a moral spectrum of professional distance with equally inappropriate expressions of human connection and disconnection at either end.

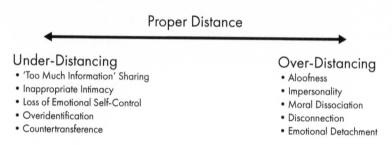

In pretty much every context, there's an extreme on either end that would be unhealthy for any human relationship. Unwelcome sexual advances are an expression of Under-Distancing. Ignoring employee mental health is an expression of Over-Distancing. So, what does the middle ground look like?

Do we really have to say that a pat on the back should be "brief" in order for it to be proper? I've got some ideas about the qualities of proper distance that I think might be helpful.

PROPER DISTANCE IS UNIQUELY INDIVIDUAL

What is considered proper physical or emotional distance depends on the context in which communication is taking place. Who you're talking to is just as important as where you are. Each person comes to a relationship or interaction with their own culture and set of values, and every environment requires slight adjustments to how those values can be expressed.

A few years ago I flew to Savannah, Georgia in the United States for a series of meetings with the Crider company. I was greeted by nearly everyone with a huge, warm hug, whether I wanted it or not. Georgia has a hugging culture, which I didn't mind since I'm a hugger myself. What I didn't expect (and threw me off a little bit) was the degree of transparency offered by strangers when I casually greeted them with "Hi, how are you doing?" I meant it to be a polite greeting, and I expected a polite response. Maybe something like "Fine. You?" But that's not at all what I got from Sharon.

In the great state of Georgia, if you ask someone how they're doing, they're likely to respond as Sharon did. "Well God bless you for asking," she said, "I can't seem to say a single thing right to my teenage son these days and I'm worried that he's not going to pass his math exam, but y'know I dare not offer him any help outta fear he's gonna jump down my throat for meddling in his business. He really is a good kid, though I wish he'd take the dog out like he's supposed to. Y'all got kids?"

PROPER DISTANCE IS DEFINED INDIVIDUALLY, THROUGH A SWIFT NEGOTIATION BY BOTH PARTIES IN AN INTERACTION.

So, I reciprocated in kind. After all, when in Rome … or Savannah. I told her about my kids and we bonded pretty quickly over the challenges of raising a teenage son.

Proper distance is defined individually, through a swift nego-tiation by both parties in an interaction, and it fluctuates based on the level of trust in the relationship. I suppose it makes sense to have some guidelines about the kinds of arenas in which proper distance might be mismatched between colleagues in a company, but ultimately, the appropriate briefness of a pat on the back from one colleague to another will be defined by those two colleagues. It will change depending on the situation (for example, whether they're alone in the breakroom or standing next to each other presenting a report to the board of directors) and their degree of mutual trust.

As gracious and loving leaders, we should try to hold space for whatever professional distance is needed by whoever we're talking to. I want people to feel as welcome and safe with me as possible, so Sharon's under-distanced response, though not in line with my values, was perfectly acceptable to me. I wasn't offended by her over-sharing, because my relationship with Sharon mattered to me.

PROPER DISTANCE IS CONTEXTUAL

As I mentioned in the stories above, my definitions of pro-fessional distance have changed dramatically depending on whether I was in Abu Dhabi, Yemen, or Georgia. It's also important to recognise that what may be appropriate social distance for someone may change between the boardroom, the breakroom, and the bar across the street. The principle at play here is to never assume that definitions of professional distance translate seamlessly from one environment to another, even in the same relationship (**FP3.3**).

I try to meet as many of my coaching clients as I can in coffee shops for this very reason. The environment is a good fit for my style of coaching, specifically because it lowers the professional distance that might be required in a boardroom, or a CXO's office. It helps encourage a more casual conversation, which usually leads to greater openness from my client and high-quality information for me. It helps me serve them better.

I also wear different kinds of clothing to signal reductions in professional distance. I wear a suit when starting a relationship with a new coaching client. I remain in a suit throughout my coaching relationship with some clients, because it signals the level of professional distance they are comfortable with. I shake hands, but I don't hug.

But after a couple of sessions with many other clients, once I've established rapport and relationship with them, I will start attending our coaching sessions in jeans, a polo shirt, and VANS. This helps to signal that I'm lowering the professional distance and equalising power. The relationship is viewed as more casual and this allows for greater openness. With many of these clients, our greetings evolve from handshakes to hugs. But each person is different, so the environment is something I curate to make my coaching more effective.

PROPER DISTANCE PROTECTS OTHERS FROM OUR VALUES

This might be the most important principle on proper distance. Sharing my personal values with someone who might not subscribe to them is dangerous ground, especially if they feel that my sharing them means they have to agree with them. And questioning or criticising someone else's values without the relational foundation of trust necessary to weather a deep conversation like that can be disastrous.

It isn't helpful for Rosalie to tell Randy that her religious beliefs are opposed to his homosexual practices. And it wouldn't be helpful for me to enter into a debate over gun control with Sharon, my newly acquired Republican friend in Georgia. She and her husband own lots of guns, and I'm a firm believer in gun control. Perhaps, after enough conversation to establish a foundation of mutual trust, I could ask Sharon her views on gun control. But I can't close that gap of professional distance existing between us without establishing trust and mutual autonomy – these are the potential bridges between our differing value systems, but they take time to build.

Power also influences perceptions of autonomy in professional distance. I was holding a million-dollar deal in my hands when I met Sharon. It wouldn't have been fair for me to open up a controversial issue like gun control while I was holding a deal like that in limbo with them. That might feel manipulative.

She might feel obligated to agree with me in order to curry my favour, and that's not authentic.

Genuine curiosity and genuine love can form a strong enough bridge for us to have conversations about opposing value systems, but again that comes with trust and time. The right to close the professional distance by exposing someone else to my opposing values is something I have to earn, and that can only occur once I am certain they can act with autonomy in the discussion.

> **GENUINE CURIOSITY AND GENUINE LOVE CAN FORM A STRONG ENOUGH BRIDGE FOR US TO HAVE CONVERSATIONS ABOUT OPPOSING VALUE SYSTEMS, BUT AGAIN, THAT COMES WITH TRUST AND TIME.**

THE RECEIVER DECIDES THE DEFINITION

The person being communicated to decides what level of emotional and physical distance is proper for them, and the communicator needs to discern that. The challenge is that sometimes the communicator won't know until they've spoken (or acted) that they've bumped into a glass wall in their communication – or even offended the person they're communicating with (**FP3.4**).

It's the receiver's responsibility to make the offence clear, allowing the communicator to adjust their distance expectations. But this doesn't always go well or produce the kind of clarity that's needed to avoid a conflict. This happens a lot when a friendly gesture is received as unwelcome attention, or when flattery is misunderstood as flirting.

For example, my wife Nicole received an email from a male colleague this morning that started with "Hi Beautiful." She was a bit taken aback. She turned to me and remarked, "That's weird. We're not 'there.' We don't have that kind of relationship."

I encouraged her to see this as just her colleague's subtle request to lower the professional distance in their relationship. If there was enough trust on her side to do that then she should; it would make the working relationship easier later on. Correcting him would establish a boundary, but it would also maintain a potentially unnecessary level of distance. Did she want a more casual working relationship or a stronger boundary? Which would be more beneficial to her?

Too often little misunderstandings can become big problems. In 2015 for example, Ellen Pao, alleged sexual harassment in her lawsuit against venture capital firm Kleiner Perkins after they fired her as CEO of Reddit. She alleged that a male colleague had made inappropriate advances towards her, and she was fired after her registering a complaint against him. Kleiner Perkins argued that Pao was dismissed for poor performance, and that the allegations of sexual harassment were just misunderstandings in communication. But how can we know? We weren't there, so we can't, and it cost the company massively, both financially and in the press.

The judge sided with Kleiner Perkins and rejected the sexual harassment claim, but the case highlighted a larger conversation about sexual harassment. It serves as a reminder that clear training and communication are essential to making sure that employees feel safe, and that exchanges intended to deepen friendships aren't misunderstood as breaches of proper distance.

CONSENT IS THE KEY

It's a simple thing to ask out loud, "Hi, how should I greet you? I'm a hugger but I'm happy to shake hands." Most people appreciate being asked, and everyone I've met is willing to be transparent about what proper distance means to them. And if you do suspect you might have taken a step too far, take a quick step back and seek clarity (**FP3.5**). For example,

> MOST OF THE TIME WE DON'T THINK TO ASK FOR CONSENT BECAUSE WE TEND TO ASSUME THAT OTHERS ARE AT THE SAME RELATIONSHIP LEVEL WITH US AS WE THINK WE ARE WITH THEM. THIS ASSUMPTION IS OFTEN MISTAKEN.

- I'm sorry, that was a bit casual. Maybe I shouldn't have said that. I'm assuming you and I are at a level of relationship where we can share stories like that. Am I right?
- Can I hug you? Is that alright?
- Can I tell you something funny that might border on inappropriate? Are we close enough for that?

- Can I sit next to you? Would that be okay?
- I can see you're upset. How can I show you some support?

How hard is that? Not really hard.

Most of the time we don't think to ask for consent because we tend to assume that others are at the same relationship level with us as we think we are with them. This assumption is often mistaken. And it's just as untrue about emotional connectedness as physical connectedness. Here are some more examples that I've heard others use:

- Can I share a story with you about my father? I want us to become better friends.
- Do you mind if I flirt with you a little?
- Can I call you Mary? Dr. Mary just seems too formal for us now.
- I just lost my mum this week and I really need to talk to someone. Would you mind?

Each of these examples seeks consent for the communicator to invite the receiver into a new kind of relationship, with less emotional distance than their relationship previously had. And ultimately this is what most people want most of the time.

If you're having an emotionally allergic reaction to this idea in light of the "flirting" example above, I know where you're coming from. I'll address the intricacies involved in hearing, understanding, valuing, and loving in communication later on, along with the context of sex, romance, and workplace sexual harassment (See Chapter 10 and Appendix B). Please bear with me for now as we explore some very challenging ideas together. I don't have it all figured out just yet, but I'm not shying away from the tough nuances either, and I think the payoff is worth the exploratory work.

What I do know is that humans are highly social animals, and we all want to feel connected to those around us, both in and out of the workplace. Stronger connections help us to feel safe, cared for, provided for and protected. It takes psychological safety to reduce proper distance, but the reduction of distance in a relationship most often leads to both parties feeling greater psychological safety as well. And who wouldn't want that?

So when in doubt, ask.

NEW POLICY: SEEK CONSENT AND RESPOND GRACIOUSLY

I think where many of our organisations have gone wrong with professional distance in recent years is that we've applied the lowest common denominator as the benchmark. We've decided that we should all adhere to the most isolating individual preferences for physical and emotional distance, as general policy, so that no member of the tribe is offended. But the side effect is that we are all afraid of connecting with each other out of fear of giving offence.

It's a bit like the emotional version of a nut-free school policy. When my daughter went to school she had a classmate with a severe nut allergy, so none of the kids could bring any food products from home that contained nuts. The needs of the one outweighed the needs of the many, because it was literally a life-or-death consideration. But the difference with professional distance is that it's not a life-or-death consideration. We need to be careful not to outlaw natural human connection because of a few members' social sensitivities.

Some people from some cultures and in some contexts might feel that a not-so-brief pat on the back is an unwelcome expression of physical contact, so just to make sure, we outlaw the back-pat for everyone in a policy manual.

Some people from some cultures in some contexts might find a particular word choice in a message to be inappropriate, so we make policies to address that. Yet no one knows exactly what that word might be in any context – so anyone might complain that any word was inappropriate to them personally.

> **I THINK WE ALL NEED TO BE A LOT MORE GRACIOUS WITH EACH OTHER.**

The result is that we're all more cautious and formal in our messages to each other than we need to be, out of fear of one person's potential sensitivity to a particular word at a particular time in a particular message. It's exhausting and terrifying. I think we all need to be a lot more gracious with each other.

I'm not saying that any person should tolerate unwanted attention from a colleague, but how can a well-meaning communicator know it's unwanted unless they've asked? Flirting is a sexual advance, and that requires consent. I am suggesting that if a colleague seeks consent to flirt, a polite "no, thank you" in response should be sufficient to clarify the boundary and avoid miscommunication. Asking for consent to flirt is not the same as flirting.

It should be the same when a colleague seeks to connect emotionally by inviting another colleague to listen to a personal story, or a fear. Seeking consent to deepen a relationship is a pre-emptive clarification tool for proper distance, and any attempt to seek consent should be celebrated, even if the consent is denied. Imagine this brief conversation:

"Hey, do you mind if I flirt with you a little?"

"I'm flattered, Tim. Thanks, but I'm not comfortable with that."

Can you imagine how much money we would save in legal costs alone if seeking consent and gracious responses were the norm?

Again, I'm not suggesting that unwanted attention should be acceptable, but I am suggesting that genuine consent seeking is a step in the right direction for determining whether that attention is "wanted," with genuine gracious response as its counterpart for a polite decline. Presumably every office romance began at some point with a single intrepid over-the-line toe-step into consent, and there are millions of true love stories that grew from this terrifyingly rocky soil. I hope I don't have to defend what should be obvious to all of us: that workplace sexual harassment has nothing at all to do with love.

In any case, we can't learn to love each other if we can't even begin to talk about love, however platonic, because it might somehow be in breach of policies and procedures.

If I sent a message to a colleague that said "I love you," it might indeed be flagged as an inappropriate message in breach of the professional distance policy. In order to get to love at work, we need to be more mature and nuanced in our understanding of proper distance.

The gap that I want to insert love into is the one created by overcautious and generalised expectations of professional distance across all cultures and contexts, which I see as a waste of human potential. Proper distance is specific to three things: the interpersonal context of those involved in the interaction, the nature of their relationship, and the environment they're in at the time.

Now that we know what we're trying to fix, we can start to look at the solution. But if love really is the solution to all of this unnatural distance, then we first need to know what we mean by love.

FIRST PRINCIPLES

FP3.1 Professional distance, though meant to facilitate multicultural collaboration, can inadvertently create barriers when generalised.

FP3.2 Proper distance safeguards others from our values.

FP3.3 Proper distance is unique and context-specific within each relationship.

FP3.4 Proper distance isn't standardised but depends on the communication recipient.

FP3.5 Proper distance can be clarified simply through seeking consent and responding graciously.

NEXT STEPS

1. Question your professional distance policy: does it really need to be as defined as it is, or is it potentially getting in the way of human connections in your organisation?
2. Reduce professional distance in your workplace relationships by seeking consent to do so.
3. Clarify your proper distance expectations graciously with those at work you feel are being too casual with you.
4. Be the kind of leader who supports connectedness at work.

THE SERCO INCIDENT

CHAPTER 4

KINDS OF LOVE

How Can Four Letters Be So Powerful,
and So Ambiguous?

"LOVE IS THE OXYGEN OF THE SOUL."

—TONY ROBBINS

THE SERCO INCIDENT

"What would it mean for you to feel loved at work?" I blurted out.

I hadn't given much thought to what I was saying, it just seemed like the right thing to say at the time, on stage, in front of the top fifty managers and executives of a major multinational company, during a day-long leadership event.

I shocked myself. It wasn't calculated; I really was just in the moment with a bunch of leaders I respected and became vocally curious about love at work. I immediately highlighted that what I'd said was inappropriate by pretending to criticise myself.

I yelled from the stage in a grumpy-old-man voice, "You can't say that, Dr. Corrie! You can't say the word love when we talk about other people at work! It's unprofessional!"

Then I laughed. So they laughed. But none of us knew where to go from there.

So I made it up as I went along.

But why not? Why can't we say love? I can say in general that I love my job, that I love my company, that I love the people I work with, but I can't use anyone's name in particular and say that I love Phil (for example). Somehow that's not allowed. It's not professional.

> I CAN SAY IN GENERAL THAT I LOVE MY JOB, THAT I LOVE MY COMPANY, THAT I LOVE THE PEOPLE I WORK WITH, BUT I CAN'T USE ANYONE'S NAME IN PARTICULAR AND SAY THAT I LOVE PHIL (FOR EXAMPLE). SOMEHOW THAT'S NOT ALLOWED.

It's one thing to say that "I love working with Greg," and an entirely different thing to say that "I love Greg, with whom I work." In the first instance it's the work that I love, and in the second, it's Greg. And we decided at some point that it's unprofessional for me to "love Greg," no matter how true it may be.

So I again asked the room packed with highly experienced senior managers:

"What it would mean for you to feel loved at work?"

And to my surprise and delight they responded.

Some said that they would be happier, others that they would work harder. Some replied that they would trust others more if they themselves felt loved in their team. And a number replied that they in fact already felt loved by some of those they worked closest with, though they wouldn't tell them so directly or say it out loud in a meeting.

What I found compelling about the discussion was how well received it was, how natural, how much it felt like a collective sigh of relief that we were finally able to say something so deeply unprofessional out loud together and just allow it to be true without providing caveats, definitions, or boundaries.

There was no need to dull the edges by saying that we weren't talking about sex, flirting, or any romantic undertone. We all knew it was what we all wanted, what some of us already experienced – and what none of us could say out loud.

Until now.

After the event, the CFO approached me to say that he was really impressed. He resonated with my ideas about the need for people in our organisations to feel heard, understood, and valued … but also with the potential for performance, loyalty, and camaraderie that would undoubtedly follow if our employees felt loved as well.

I agreed, and the next day I started writing this book.

THE CHOCOLATE-CHILD SPECTRUM

I used to be a high school sex educator in Estonia. One of the most fascinating things to me at that time was how teenagers thought about love and sex. As a part of the programme, I would ask an auditorium of often hundreds of teens, "Who thinks love and sex are the same?"

Usually about half to three-quarters of the hands would go up in agreement. To which I would respond, "Well, if love and sex are the same thing, then that's really bad for me, because I love my mother."

This would be followed by a roar of disgust-fuelled laughter. But then I reframed the discussion. I mentioned my mother as someone I could love but clearly not be interested in sexually, and I noted that the reality of sexual assault meant that it was possible to have sex completely in opposition to love.

"So if love and sex aren't the same thing," I asked, "then what is love?"

I bring this up here because I think we adults often aren't much more intellectually astute about the relationship between sex and love than my teenage students were. We've kicked the word "love" out of our professional spaces because of the potential mix-up with sex and romance. Like immature little school kids, we fear hearing "I love you" in the office, and having to immediately sort out whether or not it's intended as anything romantic.

It doesn't feel right to me that this is the case, especially in economic tribes where we spend half of our lives with each other every day. But here's where the problem lies …

Love is perhaps the most imprecise word in the English language.

> LOVE IS PERHAPS THE MOST IMPRECISE WORD IN THE ENGLISH LANGUAGE. IT'S SO VAGUE AS TO ALMOST BE USELESS.

It's so vague as to almost be useless. On one extreme I might say, "I love chocolate," or "I love Matt Damon, he's such a good actor. I mean seriously, I absolutely LOOOOOVE that guy." It doesn't matter that the chocolate can't love me back, or that Matt Damon and I have never met, it's still love.

On the other end of the spectrum I might say, "I love my kids," or "I love my wife." These are expressions of sacrificial loyalty and primary allegiance. The word love here means something totally different than it did when I used it to describe my relationship with Matt Damon, or chocolate. And with chocolate on one side and my children on the other, it's pretty easy to see that neither end of the spectrum of meanings for "love" have anything at all to do with romance or sex (**FP4.1**).

FIGURE 5:   THE CHOCOLATE-CHILD SPECTRUM

So, do you see my problem?

This is exactly why in the last fifty years of research on leadership and management, very few leaders have dared to use a word so rich with meaning and yet so unclear as the word "love."

It means everything from a casual preference to an undying commitment, and is at some point on that journey related to romance and sex (**FP4.2**). So, if we're going to use the word love in the office, we'll need a working definition that we can all agree on. Let's try to find it.

LOVE IN GREEK

Finding a definition of love would be easier if we all spoke Greek. I'm from a Christian faith background and studied a bit of Greek when I was learning to read the Bible. I learned that there are six different words in Greek that show up as "love" in English. I'll show them to you, and maybe they can help us to find shared meaning on a definition of love in the workplace.

- *Eros* is the one that gets us into trouble. It's the romantic, passionate, and often sexual expression of love. But once we have this one out of the way, there are still five more!
- *Ludus* is a playful kind of love. It's kids running around playing with each other in the back yard. It's the girls gathering for sundowners and a good laugh after work. It's what happens when I have one more cocktail than I should and I put my arm around a guy I've just met and say quite sincerely, "I love you, man."
- *Philia* is the love that resides in close friendships. It's platonic and yet committed, like lifelong besties, or brothers in arms. It's also the friend-zone, where romance is banished but care and loyalty remain. This is probably the closest to the love we are looking for in the workplace. It's mutual, platonic, caring, and committed (**FP4.3**).
- *Pragma* is the love expressed in tolerance and patience. It's the love that allows my kids to crawl on me, even when I'm tired and annoyed. It puts up with discomfort rather than asking another person to change. It's the CHRO politely

listening to the CIO talk about RPAs and APIs without interrupting her for definitions, because he trusts her.[39]

- *Agape* is unconditional love. This is the love that most parents have for their children, or the love that exists between partners in a long-term committed relationship. This is the love that many believe that God has for his creation. It is a resilient self-sacrificing love, not easily upset and very difficult to break.

- *Philautia* is love for oneself. This kind of love is the starting point for all of the others. Loving others is truly only possible from the vantage point of self-appreciation and valuing oneself. Claiming to love someone else while hating yourself isn't love, it's worship. The love you have for yourself is what makes the love you give to others meaningful.

LOVE IN ARABIC

I've spent five years living and working in Yemen, and more than a decade in Dubai, and I'm fortunate to have learned some Arabic along the way. Love is a lot easier to understand in Arabic than in English. It's a bit like Greek that way, as there are lots of words to choose from. Here are some that I think will help:

39　Robotic Process Automations (RPAs) and Application Programming Interfaces (APIs) are common tools used in digital transformation in organisations.

- حُبّ (*ḥubb*) – This is a common word for love, and it covers the entire spectrum from chocolate to children, including romance. It's like the English word for love, and you can use it when you don't want to be too specific about what you mean when you say you love someone or something.
- عِشْق (*ʿishq*) – This is a passionate, intense love. It's the romantic-spiritual connection that partners who have fallen in love feel for each other for a long time.
- غَرَام (*gharam*) – This one is similar to the last one as it refers to a romantic or amorous love, but it describes a more sexual and less spiritual connection. This might be a hot, steamy kind of love, the kind that dwindles over time as eroticism in a relationship decreases.
- وَلَع (*walaʿ*) – This kind of love expresses fondness or affection. It might also be used to describe a burning desire or longing for someone or something, or enthusiasm for a particular interest. It's less intense than *ʿishq*.
- مَحَبّة (*mahabba*) – This is a strong, deep, committed love that includes a profound sense of care and concern. It's the sacrificial love that parents have for their children, or close friends for each other. It often exists between romantic partners, but doesn't carry any sexual or romantic overtone. I think this is the one we are looking for when we talk about love at work.
- شَغَف (*shaghaf*) – This refers to a strong desire or passion for something, like an activity or a hobby. This is the love of a fan for their favourite football team. It's an intense interest, not a mere preference.

- رَمَانَة (*ramana*) – This isn't a common word. It's mostly found in ancient Arabic poetry, but I like it because it refers specifically to a love that is hidden or secret. It's a bit risqué, like what we might call a "secret crush" in English.
- تَعَلُّق (*ta'alluq*) – This love involves a close emotional attachment with someone or something, but it's unique in that it can be interpreted negatively as well. It can be a deep meaningful connection with another person, but it can just as easily be an unhealthy obsession or co-dependency.

We English speakers live in such poverty, having to sort out all of those potential meanings from a single word. In Arabic we could simply say مَحَبَّة (*mahabba*), or in Greek we would use *Philia*, and everything would be clear. I wish I had a word in English that means

"I love you ... more than chocolate and less than my children, but with a strong sense of care and commitment and no sexual or romantic overtones."

That would be ideal.

Now imagine my frustration as a leadership expert struggling to bring the richest of human experiences (love) into the context where we spend

> I WISH I HAD A WORD IN ENGLISH THAT MEANS "I LOVE YOU... MORE THAN CHOCOLATE AND LESS THAN MY CHILDREN, BUT WITH A STRONG SENSE OF CARE AND COMMITMENT AND NO SEXUAL OR ROMANTIC OVERTONES."
>
> THAT WOULD BE IDEAL.

the majority of our lives (work), having only one blunt and cumbersome four-letter tool to work with. It's like trying to read poetry through fogged glass. It's no wonder my heroes in the leadership disciplines have traditionally avoided the word altogether.

INGREDIENTS IN LOVE AT WORK

We might not have a particularly good name for love at work, but we know what it looks like. So let's look at the qualities of the kind of love that we find in the workplace and see if that helps. Here's what I see as the essential ingredients in love at work:

- Emotional Connection: People who feel love at work experience feelings of empathy, trust, and intimacy that develop to a sense of emotional connection.
- Shared Values: People who feel love at work typically connect with others that they have shared values, beliefs, and goals with.
- Positive Interactions: People who feel love at work experience fairly consistent positive expressions of affection and appreciation.
- Physical Contact: When working in the same physical environment, non-sexual expressions of physical contact, like a hug, are a common ingredient in a loving work relationship.
- Commitment: People who feel love at work are willing to work through misunderstandings, challenges, and difficulties in order to maintain a close relationship over time.

- Transparency: People who feel love at work actively listen to each other and feel safe to openly and honestly share their thoughts and feelings with each other.
- Trust: People who feel love at work do so with others that they trust, and who trust them.
- Shared Experiences: People who feel love at work often share experiences, projects, meals and other activities, and their shared hobbies and interests may extend beyond the workplace.

Look at that list (**FP4.4**). Is there anything you would disagree with? Anything you would add? If we used those ingredients to describe love at work, would we be most of the way to a complete description?

I think so.

PSYCHOLOGY OF LOVE AT WORK

One of the best-known models of love in psychology is Sternberg's triangle model (1986) that includes Intimacy, Commitment, and Passion. Intimacy is a sense of closeness and transparency with someone else. You tell them secrets, and they tell you secrets. Commitment starts with an initial decision to bond yourself to someone, and eventually becomes the long-term decision to remain bonded to them. And Passion in Sternberg's model involves physical attraction, sexual compatibility, and romance.[40] Healthy love is a blend of at least two of the three ingredients.

- If you only have Commitment, then it's an empty love. You can love someone you aren't intimate with and aren't passionate about, but it's a hollow kind of love. I've seen that in some old married couples I know.
- If you only have Intimacy, then it's a kind of strong "liking." You can love someone that you're not passionate about and not committed to, but it's just a powerful kind of preference. You like that person, a lot.
- If you only have Passion, then it's infatuation. You can be passionate about someone that you're not committed to and aren't intimate with, but then you're just infatuated.

I like this model because we can use it to isolate love in the workplace from sexuality and romance. If we get rid of Passion, then we end up on the spectrum between Intimacy and Commitment with what the psychologists call Companionate Love (**FP4.5**). I think that's a pretty close description of love at work.

---

40 Sternberg, R. J. (1986). A triangular theory of love. *Psychological review,* 93(2), 119.

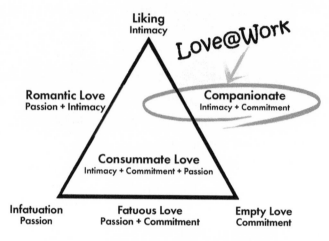

FIGURE 6: STERNBERG'S (1986) TRIANGLE MODEL

A loving relationship at work is made up of intimacy and commitment. The commitment takes place at the beginning of intimacy, when the "liking" of someone begins. You like them, so you tell them something private. They do the same, and your transparency starts to build into trust over time, leading to commitment. The commitment deepens the more the intimacy deepens, in a reciprocal relationship (**FP4.6**).

So if we want to build more loving workplaces, we should probably look briefly at how intimacy deepens in relationships, right?

Let's take Mark and Mary as examples. Let's say Mark wants to build intimacy with Mary. Mark starts by disclosing some personal feelings or information to Mary, which Mary interprets through her filters (her own hopes, dreams, and fears). Mary responds to Mark, which Mark then interprets through his filters.[41]

Now, if Mark feels understood and valued, the intimacy in the relationship will deepen. Mark's hopes and dreams for the relationship with Mary will increase, and his fears about the relationship will decrease. If Mary's response is sympathetic, then the next time Mark speaks to Mary, he'll trust her more.

But if Mark doesn't feel understood and valued by Mary's response, then his fears will increase and his hopes and dreams will decrease, and the intimacy in the relationship will be reduced. The next time Mark speaks to Mary, his disclosure will be less personal, less transparent, and less intimate.

---

41   This is based on the intimacy process model of Reis, H. T., & Shaver, P. (1988). Intimacy as an interpersonal process. *Handbook of Personal Relationships*, 367-389.

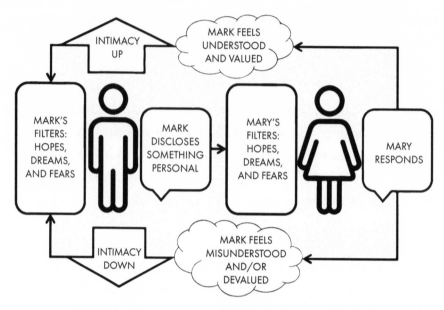

FIGURE 7: THE INTIMACY PROCESS MODEL OF REIS & SHAVER (1988)

The more Mary and Mark feel understood and valued by each other, the more intimate they will become. In psychology this phenomenon is called positivity resonance. It's a personal disclosure followed by a sympathetic response. Each person is reciprocating the transparency that the other offers, and reciprocating the trust that is built when each of them feels valued by the other (**FP4.7**). This value reciprocation over time becomes a specific kind of love: companionate love.

The impact of higher degrees of companionate love between co-workers in the healthcare industry has already been shown to result in better teamwork, higher job satisfaction, and lower emotional exhaustion.[42] The healthcare industry may be considered female dominant, so just in case you're concerned that these results don't translate into more traditionally masculine enterprises, consider that a similar study among firefighters, one of the most male-dominated industries, produced similar results.[43] Companionate love is not gender or sex biased, and its presence has been measured and shown to positively impact even traditionally competitive and generally emotionless environments such as software engineers in Silicon Valley.[44]

A WORKING DEFINITION OF LOVE

Back in my Estonian high-school sex-ed class, my crowd of horny teens was faced with a dilemma when trying to describe what love was. They had thought that love was always romantic, or sexual. The laugh I got from mentioning my love for my mother, also made them stop and think: if love wasn't what they thought it was, then what was it?

---

42   Barsade, S. G., & O'Neill, O. A. (2014). What's love got to do with it? A longitudinal study of the culture of companionate love and employee and client outcomes in a long-term care setting. *Administrative Science Quarterly*, 59(4), 551-598.

43   O'Neill, O., & Rothbard, N.P. (2017). Is love all you need? The effects of emotional culture, suppression, and work-family conflict on firefighter risk-taking and health. *Acad Manage J.*, 60(1):78-108. doi:10.5465/amj.2014.0952.

44   O'Neill, O. (2018). The FACCTs of (work) life: How relationships (and returns) are linked to the emotional culture of companionate love. *American Journal of Health Promotion, 32*(5), 1312-1315.

I challenged them to take on the seemingly impossible task of separating love from sex. When I asked for a definition they could all agree on, they would shout out words like: commitment, emotion, helping, trust, and sharing. Those words moved us in the right direction for sure, away from the meanings attached to sex and chocolate.

It generally didn't take more than a few minutes for them to reach nearly the same conclusion each and every time. It was remarkable. The wording might vary slightly, but it always ended up describing a kind of loyalty characterised by a readiness for reciprocal self-sacrifice. Something like this:

> **LOVE IS THE WILLINGNESS TO REDUCE MY QUALITY OF LIFE IN ORDER TO IMPROVE THE QUALITY OF SOMEONE ELSE'S LIFE.**

> Love is the willingness to reduce my quality of life in order to improve the quality of someone else's life (**FP4.8**).

In that definition they found something they could all agree on. It covered a relationship between a parent and child, besties in the school hallway, an owner for her dog, and partners in a long-term committed relationship. This is the definition we'll start with when discussing love at work.

You'll notice that love in this definition isn't the act of self-sacrifice *per se*, but the willingness for it. It's a state of mind. A psychological posture. Being prepared to give up something for someone else is in and of itself a loving attitude, even if the implied sacrifice is never actually needed.

BEYOND EMPATHY

I used to think it was enough for us to describe leaders as caring, considerate, empathetic, understanding, vulnerable, transparent, humanity-driven, encouraging, emotionally intelligent, people-oriented, socially aware, inclusive, respectful, and patient, but I'm no longer satisfied by that vocabulary.

Perhaps the closest concept we have to loving leadership without saying loving is empathetic. There's been a lot of talk about empathy in leadership in recent years, but it doesn't quite scratch the itch of love.

While an empathetic leader seeks to understand the feelings of others, there is no requirement of courage or commitment in empathy. A leader can be compassionate and understanding of their employees yet still lack that deeper emotional connection, that warmth, belonging and true affection for those they lead.

There are colleagues of mine who, if I met them in the office tomorrow and did not hug them tightly, might think that a breakdown has occurred in our relationship that needs to be repaired. But that level of physical and emotional connection takes time. It starts with a handshake and evolves through a series of steps before reaching the level of connectedness we now experience.

Let's turn now to the roadmap from professional distance to love at work.

FIRST PRINCIPLES

FP4.1 Love, a multifaceted term, can range from preference to profound allegiance and sacrifice.

FP4.2 Love's association with sex and romance is just one of many interpretations.

FP4.3 Non-romantic love is expressed in languages like Arabic (*mahabba*) and Greek (*philia*).

FP4.4 The ingredients in love at work are:
- Emotional Connection;
- Shared Values;
- Positive Interactions;
- Physical Contact;
- Commitment;
- Transparency;
- Trust;
- Shared Experiences.

FP4.5 Psychology terms non-romantic but intimate and committed love as "companionate love."

FP4.6 People seek non-romantic love at work, desiring care without confusion.

FP4.7 Relationship intimacy grows through personal disclosure and empathetic response.

FP4.8 Dr. Corrie defines love as the willingness to reduce one's own quality of life to improve another's.

NEXT STEPS

1. Think of people at work you love. What kind of love is it that you have for each of them?
2. Think of people at work who love you. What kind of love do you think they have for you?
3. Identify someone at work with whom you would like to deepen your relationship, and then intentionally disclose something personal about yourself and see what happens.
4. In what ways can you intentionally encourage the eight ingredients listed above in your workplace?
5. Which of the eight ingredients in love at work are the easiest for you to express in your leadership? Which are the most challenging?

CHAPTER 5

THE LEVELS OF CONNECTEDNESS

How Do We Climb Out of This Hole We've Dug
Ourselves Into?

*"LEADERSHIP REQUIRES TWO THINGS: A VISION OF THE
WORLD THAT DOES NOT EXIST, AND THE ABILITY TO
COMMUNICATE IT."*

—SIMON SINEK

RISING TO THE TOP

In 1960, John Maxwell wrote *The 5 levels of Leadership*, in which he talks about his view of the leadership progression process. It's a ladder that can be climbed from the lowest level of leadership to the highest level. The process looks like this:[45]

---

45   Maxwell, J. C. (1960). *The 5 levels of leadership*. Center Street.

PEOPLE FOLLOW YOU BECAUSE...	LEADERSHIP LEVELS
of who you are and what you stand for	PINNACLE (respect)
of what you've done for them	PEOPLE DEVELOPMENT (reproduction)
of what you've accomplished	PRODUCTION (results)
they want to	PERMISSION (relationship)
they have to	POSITION (rights)

I really like this model, and the reason I'm showing it to you is that it serves as the inspiration behind the model I'll be introducing to you in this book. I wanted to make sure that John was properly honoured for his ideas.

A few years ago I started to think deeply about what helps employees-as-followers to feel love for, and loved by, their colleagues and managers in organisations. What's the process and progression by which a person in their workplace might climb up that kind of relationship hill? How would we as leaders be able to recognise that progression and even curate the experience for our employees?

Looking at John's leadership levels above, it occurred to me that at the bottom level there's no love at all. Employees follow their leaders because they have to. They are participating in a hierarchy where they lack empowerment and perhaps even feel that they have no voice.

At the top level there is a significant expression of loyalty, belonging, trust, influence, and care that might be better abbreviated as love. John calls it respect, and I'm not challenging his definition here, only expanding on the possibility of what I think can be accomplished at that highest level. Love goes beyond respect, and I've seen love expressed both by and for leaders in organisations.

The progression from the bottom to the top, in the context of curating a loving relationship, is deeply interpersonal and founded on different kinds and qualities of communication. So, the model I've developed strays a bit from John's inspiration in this way: I want to concentrate on love as a quality in a leader-follower relationship that is not based primarily on achievement, but on communication. If love is to be the final frontier of empathy in leadership, and occupy that top spot on our leadership ladder, then the middle will need to be re-engineered.

What then are the levels of connectedness that lead to a person feeling loved?

PEOPLE FEEL CONNECTED BECAUSE...	LEVELS
their voice is an integral quality of the relationship	LOVED
their voice leads to change	VALUED
their voice is echoed back to them	UNDERSTOOD
they are listened to	HEARD
they are welcome	INCLUDED

These are then five levels of connectedness in a relationship that leads to the experience of love at work. This isn't how I think it *should* work; this is how I think it *actually* works (**FP5.1**). Without going into too much detail too soon, I want to introduce a few principles of this sequence.

A. Connectedness is a progression;
B. Connectedness is an individualised experience;
C. Connectedness is learnable;
D. Connectedness is difficult to gain and easy to lose;
E. Connectedness is an accelerant for influence;
F. Connectedness is relational, not structural.

CONNECTEDNESS IS A PROGRESSION

You have to start at the bottom in order to get to the top, and the very bottom level of connectedness is inclusion. The Gartner Inclusion Index measures inclusion as a combination of:

- Fair treatment,
- Integrating differences,
- Decision making,
- Psychological safety,
- Trust,

- Belonging, and
- Diversity.[46]

Inclusion has been studied alongside diversity for the last few decades as a necessary ingredient in a properly functioning organisation.[47] There are tens of thousands of research articles and books on the subject of diversity and inclusion in the workplace. For our purposes, I will look at inclusion as the very basic condition for the progressive path towards feeling loved at work. It's the entry level, and it's made up of two main ingredients: presence, and psychological safety. For an employee to begin to feel included, they first need to be invited and to feel safe.

INCLUSION = PRESENCE + PSYCHOLOGICAL SAFETY

People begin to feel connected because they feel welcomed. Each level of the connectedness progression starts from this basic condition; it occurs in order to grow a sense of belonging in the relationship towards the feeling of being loved. Once an employee feels welcome (present and safe), they can add their own voice to the relationship, whether as a member of a team or

---

46   Romansky, L., Garrod, M., Brown, K., & Deo, K. (2021). How to measure inclusion in the workplace. *Harvard Business Review*, 27.

47   Garg, S., & Sangwan, S. (2021). Literature review on diversity and inclusion at workplace, 2010-2017. *Vision*, 25(1), 12-22.

with an individual colleague or leader (**FP5.2**). The employee's voice becomes the trigger for some kind of acknowledgement. Once their voice is acknowledged, they have moved to the next level. They have been heard.

HEARD = INCLUSION + ACKNOWLEDGEMENT

People feel more connected when they are listened to. They've added their voice to the conversation in the form of words, an action, some piece of behaviour, a facial expression or hand gesture, a sound, or perhaps something written down. Once their communication is acknowledged, they feel heard (**FP5.3**).

> IF THE EMPLOYEE DOESN'T RECEIVE ACKNOWLEDGEMENT OF THEIR COMMUNICATION, THEY'RE LIKELY TO FEEL UNHEARD AND EXCLUDED.

If the employee doesn't receive acknowledgement of their communication, they're likely to feel unheard and excluded. If they weren't expecting a response, or if some mitigating circumstance made the lack of response reasonable, the employee might still consider themselves as included even if they weren't heard. However, it's more likely that if they add their voice to the relationship and there is no response, the employee will question their psychological safety and whether they're truly included in the relationship or community.

UNDERSTOOD = HEARD + ECHO

People feel understood when they hear their voice echoing back to them accurately (**FP5.4**). Being acknowledged for speaking doesn't mean that what you hear back reflects what you intended to say. What you're listening for is an echo, a piece of reciprocal communication that sounds a lot like what you intended to say. If what you hear back doesn't sound like what you meant, it's not an echo, it's a misunderstanding.

I've been a father for more than 22 years now, a lot of which has been in an ongoing struggle to be understood by my kids. It's not that they don't hear me, it's that we sometimes don't have shared meaning. My kids often disagree with me on the definition of what constitutes a clean room, for example.

This is the level of connectedness where most misunderstandings occur. If the echo the employee receives back doesn't sound like what they meant to say, then there is a miscommunication occurring, caused by a lack of shared meaning. It's important to get the echo right if you want someone to feel heard and understood by you. But that can be tricky.

> IT'S IMPORTANT TO GET THE ECHO RIGHT IF YOU WANT SOMEONE TO FEEL HEARD AND UNDERSTOOD BY YOU. BUT THAT CAN BE TRICKY.

Every piece of communication is a series of translations. In his book *Stuff of Thought*, Steven Pinker goes into amazing detail about how human communication takes place. People don't think in language. We learn language as babies, which means we must think in some other form before that: *concepts*. When we want to communicate something, we have to translate our concept into language. The language can be spoken (words); it can be non-verbal (a smile); or it can be artistic (a piece of music or sculpture).[48] Each of these is a form of communication that starts as a concept but is translated into a kind of language.

The communicator's intent is to use a form of language (words, gestures, music, etc.) to relay information that the receiver can take in through their senses of sight, hearing, touch, taste, and smell. The sensory data is then translated by the recipient back into a concept. In order for the communicator to feel understood, they need to receive back an echo in the form of another piece of communication that's produced by the receiver and sent back to the original communicator. It's a very complex process, and something that humans struggle daily to get right.

Interestingly, most people (most of the time) don't need other people to agree with them as much as they need other people to *understand* them. This is also true of employees in an organisation, who sometimes fight

> **MOST PEOPLE DON'T NEED OTHER PEOPLE TO AGREE WITH THEM AS MUCH AS THEY NEED OTHER PEOPLE TO UNDERSTAND THEM.**

---

48   Pinker, S. (2007). *The stuff of thought: Language as a window into human nature.* Viking.

to be heard and understood. They will usually still feel like active participants, even if their colleagues don't agree with their opinions and suggestions, as long as they feel understood. Understanding is more important to us than agreement because being together is more valuable than being right. Remember, people are social animals, and our survival doesn't depend on being individually right as much as it does on being socially together.

As every married person knows, understanding is not the same as agreement. Just because my wife understands me, and echoes back to me what I've said so I feel understood, that doesn't mean that she agrees with me or even values what I've said. This happens a lot when it's time for us to decide what to eat for dinner, a process in which my suggestions of pizza are very quickly understood and rapidly reflected back to me with a polite "no." I am heard, and my suggestion is understood, but I'm not yet valued. For me to be valued, I'll need the echo that I receive back to reflect some kind of change.

VALUED = UNDERSTOOD + MEANINGFUL CHANGE

People feel valued when their voice leads to some kind of mean-ingful change (**FP5.5**). On those rare occasions when my wife caves in and we do end up ordering a pizza for dinner, I feel valued. The echo that I hear back isn't just an acknowledge-ment of the suggestion I've made – it is also being reflected in meaningful change. Our dinner evolves from an idea, an inquiry, and a suggestion into a set of behaviours that end up in my beautiful wife clicking around on her phone for the food delivery app and asking me something like, "What do you want on it?"

So, even if an employee feels safe enough to add their voice to a relationship with their boss, and they receive acknowledgement that they've spoken, as well as an echo back to let them know that the boss has understood the suggestion – they will still need to see some kind of meaningful change on the part of the boss to feel valued. And yes, I've drawn a direct comparison between my wife and "the boss" in this analogy.

> **EMPLOYEES WILL REMAIN STUCK ON THE UNDERSTOOD LEVEL OF CONNECTEDNESS, AND WILL NOT FEEL VALUED, IF THEIR SUGGESTIONS, OPINIONS, INPUT AND INFORMATION ARE CONSISTENTLY UNDERSTOOD BUT DO NOT RESULT IN CHANGE.**

Employees will remain stuck on the Understood level of connectedness, and will not feel valued, if their suggestions, opinions, input and information are consistently understood but do not result in change. If this remains the case for an extended period of time, the employee will either change their mind on what should be done, change their communication strategy to more accurately convey their meaning, or seek other social circles in which their contribution is valued.

Inclusion is not enough. It's just the beginning. Implementing inclusion in an organisation requires organisation-wide change efforts and new processes and channels for decision making that invite input from lots of different sources, with authentic leadership at the top.[49] Only when decision-making processes sincerely invite diverse input and execute meaningful change based on those sources of information, can an organisation truly be seen as valuing its members. But being a valued member of an economic community, or being valued in a relationship, still falls short of the most powerful and influential form of human relationship: love.

LOVED = VALUED + RECIPROCITY
TIME

People feel loved when they recognise that their voice is an integral quality of the relationship. Now, I know that love is a dangerous word to use. As we've seen, love can mean anything from my preference for a particular kind of candy to the unconditional commitment of care and support that I offer my children. That's a broad spectrum of meaning for a little four-letter word, so let's get a bit more visibility on love here.

---

49   Boekhorst, J. A. (2015). The role of authentic leadership in fostering workplace inclusion: A social information processing perspective. *Human Resource Management, 54*(2), 241. Retrieved from https://www.proquest.com/scholarly-journals/role-authentic-leadership-fostering-workplace/docview/1666454004/se-2/.

In the context of evolutionary psychology, love is in part a product of altruism: a person's willingness to lower their quality of life in order to improve the quality of life for another person.[50] If the other person does the same in return, this is called reciprocal altruism. Reciprocal altruism contributes to the survival and quality of life of each person by storing potential future effort, energy, and resources in the life of another individual.

If I share my food with you today, maybe you'll share your food with me tomorrow. In that way, I can store up food for the future by feeding people today and counting on them to reciprocate my altruism later on.

> **LOVE OCCURS WHEN FEELING VALUED IS MUTUALLY EXPERIENCED OVER TIME IN RELATIONSHIPS WHERE PEOPLE CONSISTENTLY TRY TO IMPROVE THE QUALITY OF EACH OTHER'S LIVES.**

As a product of reciprocal altruism, love occurs when feeling valued is mutually experienced over time in relationships where people consistently try to improve the quality of each other's lives (**FP5.6**). That way, they're storing up value in the life of another person (or people), and they all end up living a higher quality of life than any of them could have outside of the relationship.

---

50   Krams, I. (2016). Reciprocal altruism (middle-Level theory in evolutionary psychology). In: Weekes-Shackelford, V., Shackelford, T., (eds) *Encyclopedia of Evolutionary Psychological Science*. Springer.

In the workplace, love requires consistent and reciprocal valuation, resulting in a powerful combination of

- corporate creativity,
- mutual support,
- communal identity,
- sacrificial discretionary effort,
- loyalty under strain, and
- peak performance.

When humans love one another, they offer the best of their resources, talents, and skills to a relationship with a person or community that they feel is also offering their best in return.

The experience of love comes from consistent reciprocity in a relationship that starts with inclusion (as its foundation) and is built through meaningful change over time.

CONNECTEDNESS IS AN INDIVIDUALISED EXPERIENCE

You always start at the bottom, and the speed at which you move from one level to the next will vary from person to person. I'm confident that you can name people in your life who you feel are there with you on each level. You may feel deeply loved by your partner, spouse, child, parent, sibling, or bestie, but that can't be true of everyone you know (**FP5.7**).

- You may feel valued by people in your social circles who allow your ideas to shape their views of the world, but maybe not loved by them.
- Others, like the work colleague who listens to your ideas but never likes or implements any of them might help you to feel understood, but not valued.
- The teenage daughter who acknowledges you with a casual thumbs up when you ask her for the hundredth time to please clean her room might have you feeling heard, but not understood.
- And the operations committee at work that you've been asked to sit in on (but specifically told not to speak up in) will probably leave you feeling included, but not heard.

People in your life will move up the connectedness ladder with you at different paces. Some people will connect with you quickly and move up the ladder over the course of a few conversations. Others may take months or even years of relationship to build up to a higher level of connection with you.

Some people will have biases and prejudices (such as racism) that may act as invisible barriers preventing you from progressing beyond a certain level with them. Your consistency in helping them to feel understood and valued may over time erode their defences but ultimately they will have to bring those walls down themselves to truly love you or receive love from you.

CONNECTEDNESS IS LEARNABLE

I met with Peter for the first time recently. He reached out to me on social media and invited me for a coffee to ask about starting a coaching relationship with me. I'll risk a cup of coffee with most people, but I never waste my time, and Peter learned that very quickly.

Within fifteen minutes of sitting down he was sharing many of his deepest insecurities and personal secrets with me. We reached a level of transparency and trust that he seldom experienced outside of his marriage, and I was a stranger he knew only from social media.

How can this be?

I was intentional about building connection with him. I was able to encourage Peter to move quickly from feeling *included* in this new relationship with me through the stages of feeling *heard*, *understood*, and *valued*. I listened to him, actively. I repeated back to him what I heard him saying and paraphrased it so that he felt understood. And I changed my thoughts and direction in response to his ideas.

I had no agenda with Peter, so I was able to deliver value in our relationship without forcing any of our conversation into a pre-determined narrative. We went where he wanted to go, and so he felt valued, and he received from me the value that I offered. By the end of our hour together he could see that being in a relationship with me would improve the quality of his life. I wanted to invite Peter to be a part of my life, and he wanted to do the same. It wasn't quite love at that point, but it wasn't entirely other-than love either.

What it definitely was, was intentional.

> **TAKE A MINUTE NOW AND IMAGINE YOUR LIFE SURROUNDED BY PEOPLE WHO ARE CONVINCED THAT YOUR VOICE IN THEIR LIVES IS INTEGRAL TO THE QUALITY OF THEIR HUMAN EXPERIENCE.**

I knew exactly what I wanted at the beginning of the conversation. I wanted Peter to feel as connected with me as possible, and I achieved that by offering as much connectedness to him as I possibly could.

This connectedness progression, and its ingredients at each level, comprise a set of learnable skills (**FP5.8**). You can (and hopefully will) learn to move people from one level to the next with honest intent and along a timeline that feels safe to them. Take a minute now and imagine your life surrounded by people who are convinced that your voice in their lives is integral to the quality of their human experience. That's where we're heading together.

CONNECTEDNESS IS DIFFICULT TO GAIN AND EASY TO LOSE

It takes effort to move from one level of connectedness to the next. Earning the right to love and be loved by someone, especially in a professional context, often takes a lot of time. It's an amazing thing to suddenly realise that one of your colleagues, or perhaps one of your employees, feels truly connected to you. Maybe they even feel loved by you because of how you communicate with them and treat them.

But the trust and transparency that comes with loving others, which can be so difficult to build, is unfortunately very easy to break (**FP5.9**). A careless word, unkept promise, or rejection of critical feedback can instantly knock a relationship down a level in connectedness. This can lead to feelings of hurt, betrayal, exclusion, or devaluation for both colleagues.

It's for this reason that many leaders withhold themselves in relationships and refuse to progress up the ladder with their employees. Managers often hide behind a wall of professional distance because the risk of emotional and relational cost would be too high in the rare case that they have to fire one of their employees someday. So they accept fear as their default position, curating conditions under which they can terminate their teammates without emotional pain. Tragically, that's often what encourages those same teammates, actively or passively, to sabotage their manager's success: that intentional lack of connectedness.

CONNECTEDNESS IS AN ACCELERANT FOR INFLUENCE

The more connected someone feels to you, the faster and more easily you will be able to influence them. If you love someone, and feel loved by them, then you trust them to have your best interest in mind when they ask for your help or give you a task. Employees who feel loved at work have little reason to question the judgement of an inclusive and empowering leader. And they know that if they have any concerns over a decision, a strategy, or a particular tactic, their voices will be heard, understood, and valued – because they are a loved member of their economic community.

The speed at which changes can be made is multiplied exponentially in an atmosphere of reciprocal altruism, where each member of the team is fully convinced that the team's direction is good for all members of that team (**FP5.10**). Each member then contributes to improving the quality of each other member's life in ways they could not accomplish as individuals.

There's less friction, fewer arguments, and stronger employee engagement when people feel loved at work. These conditions contribute to smoother operations, loyal talent, and higher discretionary effort, resulting in better overall performance for the firm and better business outcomes. If you love your people and your people feel loved by you, you'll all perform better.

CONNECTEDNESS IS RELATIONAL, NOT STRUCTURAL

Let's think about John Maxwell's leadership levels mentioned at the beginning of this chapter. In the model I'm describing, changes in positions or even in organisations do not affect your level of connectedness. John's levels of leadership are pinned at the bottom level to the concept of hierarchy – people follow you because they have to, because they work *for* you. Levels of connectedness, on the other hand, are not connected to any hierarchy. They are interpersonal and can occur within or outside of the official structure of the organisation (**FP5.11**).

Employees can feel loved at work through strong relationships with colleagues from other departments or other business units. They can align themselves with admired leaders outside their official reporting structure. Managers can also express loyalty and commitment to the organisation out of their love for the team that reports to them, even if they have a bad relationship with their own boss.

> MANAGERS CAN ALSO EXPRESS LOYALTY AND COMMITMENT TO THE ORGANISATION OUT OF THEIR LOVE FOR THE TEAM THAT REPORTS TO THEM, EVEN IF THEY HAVE A BAD RELATIONSHIP WITH THEIR OWN BOSS.

This relational, rather than structural, context is why people will often follow their leaders from one organisation to another. And this is why people can transform strong intra-organisational relationships into strong inter-organisational relationships later in their careers.

Colleagues in one company who develop a strong connected relationship may find themselves, for example, in a vender-purchaser relationship later on in their careers. If that happens, they'll benefit from having already laid a foundation of mutual trust and transparency that can serve to accelerate business decisions for both organisations and create synergies and competitive advantages in their industry.

How many times in your career have you heard someone at the decision-making table vouch for a stranger by saying something like, "I know her, we worked together a few years ago. She's amazing and I trust her completely," or perhaps something like, "Grant? Yes, let's get him in on this. I absolutely love that guy!"

Is it really love? Maybe not, but it's probably not other-than-love either. It's trust and respect, and it was earned in a relationship.

This happens to me quite often. Executives I train or coach in one organisation will bring me with them as a trainer or coach into their next organisation. They already know the value I provide and the genuine heart with which I serve my clients, so they shortcut the negotiation process and speed up my integration into their new company. To put it another way, they know that I love them, whether they use the word love or not, and that foundation transcends both structure and process.

A PROCESS WORTHY OF PURSUIT

This progression from feeling included to feeling heard, understood, valued, and loved is not limited to business. This is a leadership book and written for a business context, but the principles I've just outlined can be applied to any human relationship. If you want to build a better relationship with your daughter, brother, neighbour, or the guy sitting next to you on your flight to New York, this process is your trail guide from initial openness to including another human being to the ultimate expression of connectedness with them: love.

Remember that the skills of moving from one level to the next with another person are learnable. You can become more loving in your leadership, both in and outside of the office. It starts with being welcoming and inclusive, providing an atmosphere in which people can voice themselves. When you hear someone's voice, acknowledge them, and echo back to them what you've heard so they feel understood.

Allow other people's ideas to challenge and shape your own, so they will feel valued by you. Over time, the mutual exchange of value may even lead you to realise that their voice is integral. You can't imagine not having them in your life. And just like that, you've evolved from inclusion to influence, and from listening to love.

FIRST PRINCIPLES

FP5.1   Connectedness evolves from feeling included, through being heard and understood, to being valued and loved.

FP5.2   Inclusion implies psychological safety and welcome.

FP5.3   Being heard involves acknowledgement of contributions.

FP5.4   Understanding is achieved when one's intentions are echoed back.

FP5.5   Value is perceived when one's voice incites change.

FP5.6   Love is felt in a mutually contributive relationship.

FP5.7   Levels of connectedness vary across individuals.

FP5.8   Connection skills can be improved.

FP5.9   Deep connections require effort to build but may break down quickly.

FP5.10   Greater connectedness equals more influence.

FP5.11   Connectedness isn't dictated by the organisational hierarchy.

NEXT STEPS

1. Make a note of one person in your life who is at each level of connectedness with you.
2. Choose three people in your life with whom you'd like to deepen your connection. Make a note of the things that

you'll need to communicate to them in order to make that happen.

3. Reflect on your leadership style: what might you be capable of if your people loved you more as a leader?

PART TWO

MARCHING TOWARDS CONNECTEDNESS

Ch. 9: VALUED

Ch. 8: UNDERSTOOD

Ch. 7: HEARD

Ch. 6: INCLUDED

Part 2: Marching Towards Connectedness

SUITLESS IN SARAJEVO

CHAPTER 6

INCLUDED

The Very Basic, Entry-Level Starting Place
for Love at Work

*"WHY BE A STAR WHEN YOU CAN MAKE
A CONSTELLATION?"*

—MARIAM KABA, *WE DO THIS 'TIL WE FREE US*

INCLUSION = PRESENCE + PSYCHOLOGICAL SAFETY (**FP6.1**)

SUITLESS IN SARAJEVO

My venture into entrepreneurship started with the high-school sex classes in Estonia that I mentioned earlier. I was well known for writing and providing sex-ed curriculum to high schools across the country, earning the street name, "the sex guy." Though unconventional, my passion for youth work and concern for the growing HIV epidemic led me to make a difference with just my ideas.

When word of my organisation's work spread, I received a surprising call from the World Bank inviting to consult on a panel of experts in Sarajevo. I was 25. Despite feeling overwhelmed and underqualified, I accepted.

Thrown into an environment far removed from my own, I found myself in a room with top thinkers on education policy – all in smart suits, while I wore my usual hoodie and VANS shoes. It was a different world, but before the actual meeting, they made me feel welcome and safe.

They cared about my ideas and experiences, not my clothes. Thus, when it was my turn to speak, I felt secure enough to share everything I knew. Their acts of inclusion allowed me to connect and contribute, despite feeling out of place initially. Feeling included is the first step in feeling connected, even before adding one's voice to the conversation. It's about being invited, feeling welcome, and safe in a space.

> THEIR ACTS OF INCLUSION ALLOWED ME TO CONNECT AND CONTRIBUTE, DESPITE FEELING OUT OF PLACE INITIALLY.

It doesn't mean that you've yet offered anything to the community in terms of your voice; but it does mean you're in the room by invitation, and you feel welcome and safe there.

SOCIAL ISOLATION IS PAIN

As social beings, we humans have our sense of identity deeply rooted in the echo we hear back from people around us in our communities, such as:

- Our families,
- School friends,
- The kids we hang out with when we are growing up,
- The clique we identify with in high school,
- Our sub-culture in university,
- The people we hang out with on the weekend, and of course,
- The colleagues we spend the most time with at work.

In each of these groups (and there are many more), we have an identity that we are constantly presenting to our community and receiving back information about. We use the information to help us self-identify, and then we present ourselves again.

> **WE NEED OTHER HUMANS IN ORDER TO SURVIVE. IN FACT, SOCIAL ISOLATION AND FEELINGS OF LONELINESS CAN BE HARMFUL TO OUR MENTAL HEALTH, AND EVEN FATAL.**

None of us can get through this life alone. We need other humans in order to survive. In fact, social isolation and feelings of loneliness can be harmful to our mental health, and even fatal. We are such intrinsically social beings that one study found that if you're chronically lonely you're 18%

more likely to die,[51] and another found that loneliness increases our chances of dying by 27% over a 15-year period (**FP6.2**).[52]

These are terribly sobering statistics, because social isolation can happen in the workplace, during work hours, and over an extended period of time. This was the experience for millions of employees during the COVID-19 pandemic. The impact of social isolation on mental health can be devastating.

Social isolation at work occurs when the "desire of support, understanding and other social and emotional aspects of interaction have not been met."[53] It's a "lack of satisfying friendship relationships or a lack of access to social networks,"[54] or a general deficit of friends and informal interactions in the workplace.[55] Each person has a unique

---

51   O'Súilleabháin P.S., Gallagher S., Steptoe A. (2019). Loneliness, living alone, and all-cause mortality: The role of emotional and social loneliness in the elderly during 19 years of follow-up. *Psychosom Med, 81*(6), 521-526.

52   Henriksen, J., Larsen, E., Mattisson, C., & Andersson, N. (2019). Loneliness, health and mortality. *Epidemiology and Psychiatric Sciences, 28*(2), 234-239. See also Ward, M., May, P., Normand, C., Kenny, R.A., & Nolan, A. (2021). Mortality risk associated with combinations of loneliness and social isolation. *Findings from The Irish Longitudinal Study on Ageing (TILDA), Age and Ageing, Volume 50, Issue 4, July,* 1329-1335.

53   Taha, L. H., & Caldwell, B. S. (1993). Social isolation and integration in electronic environments. *Behaviour & Information Technology, 12*(5), 276-283, (p. 277).

54   Marshall, G. W., Michaels, C. E., & Mulki, J. P. (2007). Workplace isolation: Exploring the construct and its measurement. *Psychology & Marketing, 24*(3), 195-223 (p. 198).

55   Kurland N.B. & Bailey D.E. (1999). When workers are here, there, and everywhere: A discussion of the advantages and challenges of telework.

level of desire for support, informal interactions, and access to social networks in their workplace, but it's safe to say that everyone experiences these felt needs (social interaction and emotional support) and being deprived of them is a painful experience.

Pain is the brain's way of telling us that something is wrong with the world, that we are being harmed. Hold your hand too close to a flame and you'll experience pain, but you'll also feel pain by being too far removed from other people for too long. Neuroscientists say that the same areas of the brain used to process social isolation, exclusion, rejection, and loneliness are the very same as those that process and alert us to physical pain (**FP6.3**).[56] Our brains are hard-wired to experience social isolation as pain, to tell to us that something is wrong with the world – and that something needs to change in order to ensure our survival.

Mass social isolation took place during the COVID-19 pandemic. Social distancing undoubtedly saved the lives of millions

---

Organisational Dynamics, 28(2), 53-68, and Kurland, N. B., & Cooper, C. D. (2002); Manager control and employee isolation in telecommuting environments. *The Journal of High Technology Management Research, 13*(1), 107-126. See also Sahai, S., Ciby, M. A. & Kahwaji, A. (2020). Workplace Isolation: A systematic review and synthesis. *International Journal of Management 11*.

56   Eisenberger, N. I. (2015). Social pain and the brain: Controversies, questions, and where to go from here. *Annual Review of Psychology, 66*, 601-629, and Eisenberger, N. I. (2012). The pain of social disconnection: Examining the shared neural underpinnings of physical and social pain. *Nature Reviews Neuroscience, 13*(6), 421-434.

of people, yet it came with negative side effects. Millions suffered the psychological effects of loneliness and isolation. Those with clinical symptoms of anxiety, depression or PTSD were highly likely to report loneliness, poor sleep quality, and reduced ability to manage emotions.[57]

> **THE SAME AREAS OF THE BRAIN USED TO PROCESS SOCIAL ISOLATION, EXCLUSION, REJECTION, AND LONELINESS ARE THE VERY SAME AS THOSE THAT PROCESS AND ALERT US TO PHYSICAL PAIN.**

Loneliness and isolation are kinds of pain. They indicate to us that something is not right with our experience of the world. We all need to be connected, and since half of our waking lives are spent at work each day, being connected at work is a necessary part of our human experience. As we have seen, it might just be a matter of life and death.

WORKPLACE DIVERSITY, EQUITY AND INCLUSION

Let me preface this section by saying that if all of our organisational leaders were already adept at loving leadership and applied love in the workplace in a practical way, we wouldn't have to talk about DEI (Diversity, Equity & Inclusion) at all.

---

57 Bzdok, D., & Dunbar, R.I.M. (2022). Social isolation and the brain in the pandemic era. *Nat Hum Behav* 6, 1333–1343.

The reason we don't have to talk about the propriety of physical violence in the workplace (for example) is that our leaders have already led us out of that discussion. We don't really need to mention anymore that punching a co-worker in the face is inappropriate, and when it happens, we're all quick to say that it's an anomaly and not the rule. I think the same might happen with DEI initiatives once all leaders embrace love at work. But since DEI is such a huge focus these days, it seems an appropriate place to begin a conversation about love.

The path towards a more loving workplace starts at the very basic level of inclusion. And to stretch ourselves in our ability to be inclusive, we'll need to extend an invitation to welcome people who are very different from us. Diversity, Equity and Inclusion (DEI) go hand in hand in organisational development, and together they provide a strong platform that we can stand on to develop and defend a more loving workplace.

The United Nations agency responsible for DEI is the International Labour Organisation (ILO). They work towards "the right of all human beings, irrespective of race, creed or sex, to pursue both their material well-being and their spiritual development in conditions of freedom and dignity, of economic security and equal opportunity."[58] Their most recent study

---

58   The ILO conventions addressing non-discrimination and equality of opportunity and treatment in employment include: Equal Remuneration Convention, 1951 (No. 100); Discrimination (Employment and Occupation) Convention, 1958 (No. 111); Workers with Family Responsibilities Convention, 1981 (No. 156); Vocational Rehabilitation and

found that an employee's level in the enterprise hierarchy is a bigger differentiating factor on the experience of inclusion at work than an employee's background or personal characteristics. Full inclusion and the business benefits of inclusion, including increased productivity, commitment, innovation and well-being, are predominately being realised for employees at the most senior levels.[59]

What that means is that race and sex aren't as strong as income and benefit disparity in employee perceptions of inclusion (**FP6.4**). An employee who feels they're not getting paid fairly is more likely to feel excluded than one who is a member of a racial or gender minority.

Authors De Aquino and Robertson (2018) define workplace inclusion as "a sense of belonging and the ability to contribute fully and authentically to the workplace without having to hide aspects of oneself." They say that inclusion is bigger than diversity, and it involves not just who is present in the organisation,

---

Employment (Disabled Persons) Convention, 1983 (No. 159); Indigenous and Tribal Peoples Convention, 1989 (No. 169); Maternity Protection Convention, 2000 (No. 183); HIV and AIDS Recommendation, 2010 (No. 2000); and Elimination of Violence and Harassment in the World of Work, 2019 (No. 190).

59   Shapiro, G. et al., Transforming enterprises through diversity and inclusion, ILO. Geneva. Retrieved from https://policycommons.net/artifacts/2363756/transforming-enterprises-through-diversity-and-inclusion/ on 30 Mar 2023.

but how they feel, how they are treated, and how they are able to participate in achieving the organisation's goals.[60]

The impact of DEI on the bottom line is also well established now. Back in 2015, McKinsey reported that across 366 public companies in the UK, the US, Canada and Latin America,

- Companies in the top 25% for ethnic diversity were, 35 % "more likely to have financial returns above their respective national industry medians," and
- The top 25% in gender diversity were 15% more likely to outperform their peers.[61]
- Three years later, the gender diversity effect rose from 15 to 21%, and then again to 25% in the 2020 study (**FP6.5**).[62]

What this means is that companies with more ethnic and gender diversity make more money than their competitors, a lot more! And the profitability of gender balance is actually accelerating over time.

---

60   De Aquino, C. T. E., & Robertson, R. W. (2018). *Diversity and inclusion in the global workplace.* Springer.

61   Hunt, V., Layton, D., & Prince, S. (2015). Diversity matters. *McKinsey & Company, 1*(1), 15-29.

62   Hunt, V., Prince, S., Dixon-Fyle, S., & Yee, L. (2018). Delivering through diversity. *McKinsey & Company, 231*, 1-39. See also Dixon-Fyle, S., Dolan, K., Hunt, V., & Prince, S. (2020). Diversity wins: How inclusion matters. *McKinsey & Company, 6*; Cain, A. (2021). The business case for diversity and inclusion in the workplace. *Australian Restructuring Insolvency & Turnaround Association Journal, 33*(2), 34-37.

> **COMPANIES WITH MORE ETHNIC AND GENDER DIVERSITY MAKE MORE MONEY THAN THEIR COMPETITORS, A LOT MORE! AND THE PROFITABILITY OF GENDER BALANCE IS ACTUALLY ACCELERATING OVER TIME.**

Boston Consulting Group (BCG) measures inclusion in their BLISS Index (Bias-Free, Leadership, Inclusion, Safety, and Support). They found that inclusion, when done well, can cut attrition in half, as employees who feel free to be their authentic selves at work are 2.4 times less likely to quit.

When employees believe that DEI programming is a priority in the workplace, the number of all employees who are happy increases by 31 percentage points and the number of both women and men who feel motivated increases by nearly 25 percentage points.[63]

The data is clear, and yet so many of our leaders just aren't seeing it yet. Perhaps that's why 72% of the 5,000 respondents in the 2018 Deloitte study said that we need a new definition of "leader" in today's more inclusive, more empathetic, more diverse world.[64] That's three out of every four people saying we need to define leadership differently. And I am one of them.

---

63   Novacek, G., et al. (2023). Inclusion isn't just nice, it's necessary. How a survey quantifying the responses of more than 27,000 employees proves the business value of inclusion. *Boston Consulting Group*.

64   Delloitte, Female Quotient. (2018). Redefining Leadership. *The Inclusion Imperative*.

This book is my contribution.

We know inclusion works on the bottom line. Love is where I think it should take us.

INCLUSIVE LEADERSHIP

What kind of leadership do we need now to leverage the competitive advantage of inclusion? Well, the science is clear: culture change must start at the top. If the Executive Committee members aren't leading this conversation, it will have very limited impact (**FP6.6**). The researchers at BCG have some initial findings on the conditions under which DEI is most effectively implemented:

1. Senior leadership is diverse.
2. Senior leaders openly and publicly commit to DEI.
3. Managers commit to DEI and psychological safety on their teams.
4. The work environment is respectful and free of discrimination and bias.[65]

That's right. The only way to do it is for the Executive Committee, the CEO, and the Board of Directors to get it done. If you're a leader in your organisation and you're not willing to

---

65   Novacek, G., et al. (2023). Inclusion isn't just nice, it's necessary. How a survey quantifying the responses of more than 27,000 employees proves the business value of inclusion. *Boston Consulting Group.*

value DEI, then you're reading the wrong book. We're only on level 1 here. But let's assume you're on board with the science and ready to make a difference.

How, you ask?

One of the most accessible tools for leaders looking to make a difference and be the change they want to see is in the *Inclusion Nudges Guidebook: Practical Techniques for Changing Behaviour, Culture & Systems to Mitigate Unconscious Bias and Create Inclusive Organisations* by Nielsen and Kepinski. It's a great start. The authors categorise what they call "inclusion nudges" into three areas:

1. **Feel the Need** – Targeting motivation through an emotional connection. This is when an employee or a decision maker has insight on the value of DEI.
2. **Framing** – Targeting perception through applying an alternative frame. This is when unconscious biases are shifted to more positive and inclusive paradigms.[66]
3. **Process** – Targeting ability and simplicity through easy processes. This is when a default setting or process is changed to allow for less biased, more objective feedback.

Throughout this chapter, I have heavily leveraged these "nudges" to try to engage you to see inclusion as the foundation

---

66   Nielsen, T. C., & Kepinski, L. (2016). Inclusion nudges guidebook: Practical techniques for changing behaviour, culture & systems to mitigate unconscious bias and create inclusive organisations. *CreateSpace*.

of psychological safety – that first step that allows you as a leader to start moving up the connectedness ladder with your team. I'll show you how I implemented the three nudges:

1. The entire section called *Social Isolation Is Pain* above was designed to trigger you to **feel the need** of inclusion and connectedness as the appropriate response to the devastating effects of social isolation and loneliness-as-pain. Did it work? Did you see how damaging social isolation is for people? Good.

2. I then **framed** DEI as not only a sociological nice-to-have for those who need it, but a competitive financial advantage for all organisations. I translated DEI from something that was just and fair into something that might hit you right in the KPI, profit.

3. And finally, I'm hoping that the 5-level connectedness progression that you are learning about now will replace whatever **process** model you're currently using to build relationships in the workplace.

There, those are the three DEI nudges in action, right here in this book.

IF YOU WANT TO BE INCLUDED, BE INCLUSIVE

Ultimately, inclusion improves employee engagement and talent retention, and it's got a well-established bottom line impact on profitability. DEI is the thing you should do if you're greedy and competitive and you want to make more money. If you're not pursuing DEI, it's because you're protecting something that you value even more than your net profit.

> DEI IS THE THING YOU SHOULD DO IF YOU'RE GREEDY AND COMPETITIVE AND YOU WANT TO MAKE MORE MONEY. IF YOU'RE NOT PURSUING DEI, IT'S BECAUSE YOU'RE PROTECTING SOMETHING THAT YOU VALUE EVEN MORE THAN YOUR NET PROFIT.

It's profitable and important, but inclusion is also just the foundation. It's Level 1 on the connectedness progression, where you invite others into a relationship with you, as a leader, or with your organisation as an economic community.

Over the next few chapters, I'll clarify the process of moving from one stage to the next in the levels of human connectedness – concluding with a model for love in leadership in the last chapter. Once the foundation has been laid, once you've invited someone to the table and included them, well, you've still only scratched the surface of potential. The next step is to hear what they have to say. If you've laid the foundation of inclusion right, they'll definitely tell you.

FIRST PRINCIPLES

FP6.1 INCLUSION = PRESENCE + PSYCHOLOGICAL SAFETY

FP6.2 Extended isolation or marginalisation can lead to severe mental health issues or even be fatal.

FP6.3 As social beings, humans perceive social isolation as pain, due to survival needs.

FP6.4 DEI mainly focuses on ethnic and gender aspects, yet income inequality is most obvious to employees.

FP6.5 Proactive DEI approaches result in 25% higher profits compared to non-DEI peers.

FP6.6 Successful DEI implementation requires initiation from top leadership.

NEXT STEPS

1. Read Nielsen and Kepinski's 2016 book *Inclusion Nudges Guidebook: Practical Techniques for Changing Behaviour, Culture & Systems to Mitigate Unconscious Bias and Create Inclusive Organisations.*

2. Make a conscious decision now to make more money by including different kinds of people on your team.

3. Think about the people you work with, especially those who report to you: do they feel welcomed by you? Would they say the atmosphere you create at work is a safe space? What changes can you make to improve yourself as an inclusive leader?

4. Select employees with a demonstrated value of diversity.

5. If you want to help your people feel safe with you, start with your own thoughts. Try saying one of these mantras to yourself every time you look at a member of your team:

- My office is a welcoming place.
- I am only as strong as my team.
- What makes us different makes us money.
- We all add value to our shared vision.
- We all belong here.
- Each person's voice is valuable.

I HEAR DEAD PEOPLE

CHAPTER 7

HEARD

Just Because You're Talking,
Doesn't Mean Anyone Is Listening

*"WHEN WE LISTEN TO SOMEONE, THEY RECEIVE OUR
ATTENTION LIKE A GIFT."*

**–HEATHER R. YOUNGER, *THE ART OF ACTIVE
LISTENING***

HEARD = INCLUSION +
ACKNOWLEDGEMENT (**FP7.1**)

I HEAR DEAD PEOPLE

Those closest to me know that I'm a history buff. I get a kick out of reading very old and obscure texts. In fact, my first doctoral degree was a comparative literary study of manuscripts from the 7th and 8th centuries. I was living in Yemen at the time and became very curious about the divide between Eastern and Western cultures, and where the breakdown of communication happened between the early Islamic and Byzantine empires.

Yes, I get it, it's a weird thing to be curious about, but I decided to scratch my itch with a PhD.

Reading ancient texts gave me a window into how people thought about things many centuries ago. And since there was no printing press, and paper was a luxury item, it's highly likely that only very few people in each author's lifetime actually read their work. The texts were meant to hold and communicate ideas across time and distances, but I don't imagine these ancient authors could have conceived of exactly how far, or for how long, their texts would travel.

Then suddenly they found me. In preserved ancient texts I got to hear the voices of authors from hundreds of years ago. Through the passage of time, past wars and revolutions, the births and deaths of empires, suddenly there I was, hearing their voices once again. It was a very powerful idea, that I could hear these authors' thoughts, and an even more powerful one that they might hear each other's.

I decided to run a thought experiment. After having read twenty or thirty ancient texts, by authors separated over hundreds of years and thousands of kilometres, I decided they should meet one another. Of course, it would have been impossible for most of them to have known about the existence of the others when they were alive, but that didn't matter. *I* knew. I had gathered all of their available thoughts into my own head. I had given each of them a voice, imagined each of their faces, and on the blank canvas of my imagination I had them all sit down together in a circle of chairs so they could meet one another.

Sometimes two of them had competing ideas, and they needed to talk it out. So I'd have them face each other, argue, and try to seek mutual understanding even if they'd never reach an agreement. But the miracle wasn't that they could agree with each other, it was that they could hear each other, perhaps for the very first time in all of history. I imagined their conversations, their shared or contentious ideas, and I imagined them hearing each other the way that I heard them. Their conversations became my thesis.

Mediums like written texts, oral histories, songs, and in more modern times recorded music, speeches, movies, television programs, podcasts, and blogs have provided a way for people to speak so that they can be heard across centuries. Not only did I hear those authors from centuries ago, but now with the publication of my PhD thesis in the form of a book, I have positioned my voice so that I can be heard that way too, centuries from now.

> NOT ONLY DID I HEAR THOSE AUTHORS FROM CENTURIES AGO, BUT NOW WITH THE PUBLICATION OF MY PHD THESIS IN THE FORM OF A BOOK, I HAVE POSITIONED MY VOICE SO THAT I CAN BE HEARD THAT WAY TOO, CENTURIES FROM NOW.

Sometimes I wonder if 300 years from now, some digital archaeologist somewhere might search about a subject that I've written about, and stumble upon one of my texts. Perhaps they will like what I've written in *Love@Work* and revive it in their own thoughts. And maybe they'll watch one of my ancient YouTube videos to put a face and voice to the text, so they can imagine me saying it. And then, long after my children's children's children have forgotten my name … I will still be heard.

But not everyone gets to feel as heard as my dead friends and I do.

MIKE THE INTERRUPTER

Mike's the Chief Operations Officer (COO) of a major company. He's responsible for an operation that includes more than 5,000 employees and a billion US dollars in annual revenue. But his people avoid him. His direct reporting managers groan and sigh in disgust when they see that he's put a meeting with any of them in their calendar at work. They roll their eyes in solidarity and look over to each other and say something like, "I've got a meeting with Mike tomorrow, can I borrow some tape for my mouth?" – to which the others laugh. They all know.

There's no point in talking in a meeting with Mike.

Mike the Interrupter is insecure. He has a psychological need to feel like he's the most competent person in the room, and his track record of promotions only adds weight to his belief that there's nothing of real value that he can learn from those working under him in his company. So as soon as one of his team members starts talking, he figures out what they're about to say, formulates a response, and blurts it out right in the middle of them saying it. It's all in the interest of efficiency, of course [*insert sarcastic eye roll*]. Mike's a busy guy and he doesn't have time to waste listening to things he thinks he already knows.

JANICE THE IGNORER

Janice is the Senior Vice President (SVP) of HR in a company of 4,000+ employees with half a billion dollars US in assets. But her people avoid her. "She's a terrible manager," they openly say to each other behind her back. Whenever her team members give her a piece of unfavourable information, try to correct her on something, or suggest an approach that's different from hers, she ignores them. When one of her managers scheduled a meeting to confront her about the salary inequity on her team, Janice took the day off to avoid the meeting.

Janice the Ignorer is insecure. She interprets every difference of opinion as a conflict, and she hates conflict. So she avoids it by simply not responding when challenged or corrected, or by simply not turning up to the office if she suspects a potential confrontation. She lacks the humility and self-awareness to accept that maybe she too will make mistakes and sometimes she doesn't have all of the relevant information. She perceives disagreement as a threat, so she avoids it.

FEELING UNHEARD

Being included on the team doesn't automatically mean your voice will be heard. What Mike and Janice have in common (and they are both real people, BTW) is that they foster a culture of feeling unheard in the workplace. Their behaviours, interrupting and ignoring, are equally effective at showing people that their opinions and information are irrelevant. Their teams feel unheard as a direct result of these leaders' styles of communication.

A study of 4,000 employees across eleven countries found that 86% of employees feel that people at their workplace are not heard fairly at work, and they're aware that it affects their performance. Sixty-three per cent of employees feel ignored by their manager,

> 63% OF EMPLOYEES FEEL IGNORED BY THEIR MANAGER, AND 35% FEEL THAT THEIR MANAGER DOESN'T CARE ABOUT THEM AS A PERSON.

and 35% feel that their manager doesn't care about them as a person (**FP7.2**).[67]

67   UKG. (2021). The heard and the heard-nots. Retrieved from https://workforceinstitute.org/wp-content/uploads/The-Heard-and-the-Heard-Nots.pdf.

Employees who feel unheard experience feelings of rejection and exclusion, and most dangerously for the organisation, they stop speaking up. Employees who feel unheard at work are also much less likely to help out with any organisational change and development,[68] and they're much more likely to be looking for another job.[69] Employees who feel unheard often tell me things like:

> I really do want to feel like I'm part of the team, but it just seems like everyone is too busy to listen to me. I'd like to think that even the executives might want to speak with me sometimes, but after two years here, I'm pretty sure they don't even see me. Sure, I'm here, but does it matter to anyone that it's me that's here? I feel pretty invisible most of the time. Maybe it's me, maybe I really am almost useless.
>
> –JUAN PABLO, ANALYST

> My manager is an idiot. He keeps saying in the team meetings how he wants us to come up with ideas for how to make things better around here, but it's all talk. I must have sent him a dozen emails with suggestions for stuff, but do you think he did any of it? Nothing. He didn't even respond. I gave up.
>
> –SHARON, MARKETING EXECUTIVE

---

68   Morrison, E. W., & Milliken, F. J. (2000). Organisational silence: A barrier to change and development in a pluralistic world. *Academy of Management Review, 25*(4), 706-725.

69   UKG. (2021). The heard and the heard-nots. Retrieved from https://workforceinstitute.org/wp-content/uploads/The-Heard-and-the-Heard-Nots.pdf.

I was told that I'd have full managerial control, but that turned out not to be true. A lot of the best practices I'm bringing in, like a coaching culture, DEI, and investments in innovation, they scrubbed immediately. They didn't even want to hear it. It's like the Chairman doesn't understand business at all. I'm probably not going to stay long.

–RICHARD, CEO

No one really talks to me here. Honestly weeks can go by without anyone saying so much as "hi" to me.

–RAJESH, JANITOR

I don't even know why they hired me. The CFO (Chief Financial Officer) and CEO (Chief Executive Officer) clearly don't like me at all. In the first few months I brought a lot of ideas for change to the Executive Committee and they vetoed nearly everything without any explanation at all. I feel completely powerless, and stuck. This place is never going to change.

–ANNE, CHRO

Feeling unheard or unseen can stretch from the breakroom to the boardroom. Sometimes employees interpret these feelings as a reflection on them personally and their value as a person in the community. They think of themselves as "not good enough" or unworthy of attention. In a study of young workers who felt lonely, isolated, ignored, and overlooked at work, researchers found that

The sad irony … of not having a voice or feeling invisible at work is that young lonely workers may not gain the experience of interpersonal and group interactions that might foster social skill development as they mature in their working lives. As a result, they may develop less skill in appropriately disclosing their experiences of relational deficiency, further reinforcing their distress and heightened sense of social threat.[70]

When voices like those of Juan Pablo, Sharon, and Anne are ignored or shut down, the organisation loses access to their talent, and when young workers are silenced, their lack of social development might last their whole careers. In any case, the passion and creativity that we hired them for is quickly stifled, like a flame under a wet blanket, by a lack of response from leadership.

> **THE TRAGEDY IS THAT UNHEARD EMPLOYEES TEND TO DO EXACTLY WHAT THEY FEEL THEY'VE BEEN TOLD TO DO: THEY "SHUT UP."**

The tragedy is that unheard employees tend to do exactly what they feel they've been told to do: they "shut up." And that means that the creativity and innovation that they might have contributed to the community is lost, likely for

---

70 Wright, S. L., & Silard, A. G. (2022). Loneliness in young adult workers. *International Journal of Environmental Research and Public Health,* *19*(21), 14462. (p. 6).

the remainder of their time in their respective companies, possibly for the rest of their lives.

FEELING HEARD

Keep in mind that we're only on level two of the five levels of connectedness here. Most of what's been written about listening in leadership and management is about "active listening," which is listening specifically for the sake of understanding. But we're not even there yet. Active listening only starts after someone has been acknowledged.

I don't want us to get ahead of ourselves or brush over the steps that lead up to active listening and being understood. What I want to focus on here is this: if we want our employees to feel heard, they need to detect some kind of receiver for them to speak to, and they need to feel safe to use their voice.

Feeling heard is connected to psychological safety, but they're not the same thing. Psychological safety is when an employee feels the freedom to speak up whether they think their voice will be listened to or not. Feeling heard is the "belief that the content of one's voiced ideas or questions will be recognised and responded to." (**FP7.3**)[71]

---

71   Kerrissey, M. J., Hayirli, T. C., Bhanja, A., Stark, N., Hardy, J., & Peabody, C.R. (2022). How psychological safety and feeling heard relate to burnout and adaptation amid uncertainty. *Health Care Management Review, 47*(4), 308-316.

For employees to feel heard, they first need to feel that they have the right to speak. Companies can do this best by opening a lot of different communication channels for employees to add their voices to the organisation. Here are a few suggestions that I've seen work well:

- Regular one-on-ones with their direct line manager, in which the manager spends at least 70% of their time listening,
- Regular team or department meetings with an open agenda,
- Out-of-office social gatherings where employees may feel more comfortable to share information in an informal environment,
- Specific email addresses or online portals in the company where employees can submit suggestions or complaints,
- Invitations to employees to submit ideas for process improvements or innovations,
- Employee surveys to gather feedback.

Researchers are telling us that employees who feel heard at work are,

- More likely to make ethical decisions,[72]
- More committed to the organisation,[73]

---

72 Detert, J. R., Trevino, L. K., & Sweitzer, V. L. (2008). Moral disengagement in ethical decision making: A study of antecedents and outcomes. *Journal of Applied Psychology, 93*(2), 374-391.

73 Janssens, M., Sels, L., & Van den Brande, I. (2003). Multiple dimensions of communication and their influence on employee commitment. *Journal of Business and Psychology, 17*(3), 377-390.

- More ready and willing to participate in organisational change,[74]
- More likely to share information (**FP7.4**).[75]

Organisations whose employees feel heard also tend to make more money.[76]

So can we agree that helping employees to feel heard at work is a basic level of care that should be provided by all managers?

Great.

Well, if they're going to feel heard, it means someone is going to have to be listening. For most managers this is not as easy as it sounds.

MAKING TIME TO HEAR

We're living in a time of unprecedented demands and expectations, distractions and interruptions, targets and goals – and most of them are good things. My personal challenge these

---

74   Rafferty, A. E., Jimmieson, N. L., & Armenakis, A. A. (2013). Change readiness: A multilevel review. *Journal of Management, 39*(1), 110-135.

75   Ashford, S. J., & Cummings, L. L. (1983). Feedback as an individual resource: Personal strategies of creating information. *Organisational Behaviour and Human Performance, 32*(3), 370-398.

76   UKG. (2021). The heard and the heard-nots. Retrieved from https://workforceinstitute.org/wp-content/uploads/The-Heard-and-the-Heard-Nots.pdf.

days isn't that I'm sorting out the good things from the bad when deciding what to do with my day, it's that all of the things I think I need to do are good, and I can't possibly do them all.

There are simply more good things for me to do every day than can ever be done. And for many leaders, carving out the time required to help a colleague or employee to feel heard fits into that category of good things that can't be done.

And let's face it, we would all be great managers if it wasn't for our employees, right?

(just kidding!).

Okay, so here's what you can do to help your colleagues feel heard at work.

1. Block specific time for listening

My recommendation as a coach is that managers should have a communication touchpoint with each of their direct reports every day, a weekly face-to-face conversation, and a monthly team or department town hall meeting. Each of these types of connection offers different conditions for an employee to feel safe to speak up. All of them should be written into your calendar before it fills up with other "urgent" matters, or they risk being forgotten.

2. Seek and invite feedback

Consider asking your employees how they're doing and if they have everything they need. If you position yourself as a service provider to them, they'll be much more likely to feel safe enough to use their voice when they need to. Remember that the information that you need to make high quality decisions is often sitting in the minds of your team members. If they feel unsafe or disempowered, they'll punish you by not sharing it, and you'll suffer by making bad decisions.

3. Have specific ongoing open channels

Tell your people how and when they can reach you. Regular meetings will give them a specific time and place to look forward to, but if they feel something might be urgent, how should they communicate with you? Phone call, email, WhatsApp message? Make sure they know how to best get the information they have into your input channels.

4. Batch your communications

To make your time more efficient, put similar kinds of requests and communications together. For example, read and reply to all of the vacation requests at the same time, or gather all of those who want better coffee in the breakroom together at once. Batching people into conversations can help you to avoid repeating them, and it can help you sort through and prioritise whom you need to listen to first.

Respond to all of your incoming messages at specific times of the day: i.e. morning, lunch, and afternoon, in three clear batches. I do this with WhatsApp, on which I typically get around 100+ requests for conversation every day. I have set times in the early morning, midday, and in the afternoon when I respond to as many as I can. If you know me well, you'll know that I'm typically unreachable after about 7 pm.

5. Clarify time expectations

When you have a meeting with an individual or a team, let them know at the beginning how much time you've allotted for it. An employee with an hour-long explanation leading up to a request for change will feel unheard if you rush them to the conclusion at the 30-minute mark. I find a quick alignment of expectations helps, something like: "Hey, great to see you! I've got 30 uninterrupted minutes for you, will that be enough?"

6. Be completely focused

Try putting your phone away. Not just on silent, but out of view. And while you're at it, consider getting rid of your smart watch. Honestly, those things are engineered to ensure that you will be distracted as often as possible, and that every distraction will be perceived as important.

If your goal is to help whoever you're speaking with feel heard, then there are three things you absolutely cannot do: do not interrupt the person you are listening to, do not allow external interruptions to hijack the conversation, and do not get internally distracted.

7. Express gratitude for their voice

This is extremely important. No matter what information you receive, what condition it's in, what tone of voice or word choice is used, and regardless of whether you agree with it or not: if you want the other person to feel heard, your initial response should always be gratitude. I find that a simple "Thanks for sharing that," or "I hear you," is all that it takes for the other person to feel heard.

You'll notice that none of these seven steps includes you agreeing with your employee or giving them what they want. And you can get through all of these steps with your manager or colleague and still feel completely misunderstood. This is just the baseline for helping others to feel heard by you.

IF YOU WANT TO BE HEARD, LISTEN

One of the things that comes more naturally to leaders as we age is recognising the value of speaking last. I've noticed that in most Arabic boards of directors, the chairman may be perceived as autocratic, but their decisions often come after a healthy round of debate to which they themselves haven't contributed.

> THE MORE TIME WE SPEND TALKING, THE LESS WE HAVE FOR LISTENING.

Instead, they listen, sometimes for a long time. In doing so, they benefit from all of the most relevant available information in the room being presented before they say anything. It's no longer as valuable to be the smartest person in the room as it is to be the last to speak.

The more time we spend talking, the less we have for listening (**FP7.5**). As leaders in our organisations, it's the people around us – colleagues, employees, managers, customers, vendors, and partners – who have the information we need to make effective decisions. To get that information, we need each of them to feel included and acknowledged. That's when they'll feel safe and welcome to speak, and that's our richest source of information. That's why the wisest speaks last, and listens for understanding.

FIRST PRINCIPLES

FP7.1   HEARD=INCLUSION+ACKNOWLEDGEMENT

FP7.2   Sixty-three per cent of employees feel ignored by their manager, and 35% feel that their manager doesn't care about them as a person.

FP7.3   Psychological safety occurs when people feel they can speak, but feeling heard occurs when they believe someone is listening.

FP7.4   Employees who feel heard make better decisions and share more information.

FP7.5   The more time we spend talking, the less we have for listening.

NEXT STEPS

1. Carve out time for listening to people.
2. Seek and invite feedback.

3. Have specific ongoing channels open so people can always voice themselves.
4. Batch your communications to make your feedback more efficient.
5. Clarify time expectations so you know how much time is allotted.
6. Be completely focused when you are listening to someone.
7. Express gratitude for peoples' voices, even if you don't agree with them.

A SUBTLE SLIGHT

CHAPTER 8

UNDERSTOOD

What's That You Say? Your Opinion Matters?

"HEARING IS PASSIVE. LISTENING IS ACTIVE.
THE BEST LISTENERS FOCUS THEIR ATTENTION AND
RECRUIT OTHER SENSES TO THE EFFORT."

—KATE MURPHY, *YOU'RE NOT LISTENING*

UNDERSTOOD = HEARD + ECHO (**FP8.1**)

A SUBTLE SLIGHT

Peter is the SVP of Operations in a company with more than 5,000 employees. He reports to the COO, along with the SVP of Safety, which used to be Henry. One of Henry's direct reports was Shirley, Senior Manager of Safety for the company. When the last COO resigned a few years ago, Henry, the former SVP of Safety, was promoted into the position. Shirley wasn't experienced enough to step into Henry's SVP role, and it was decided that the company would keep the SVP of Safety role vacant for the time being.

But if the SVP of Safety position was to remain vacant, who should Shirley report to? Since Henry and Shirley were used to working together, maybe it made sense just to keep Shirley reporting to Henry as COO. But structurally, Senior Managers should report to a VP or SVP, not directly to a C-Suite position, so Peter decided to help out.

It made sense to Peter that Shirley should report to him, and not directly to the COO. Peter was quite capable and competent to oversee Shirley in her role, and shifting the reporting line from the SVP of Safety to the SVP of Operations could potentially eliminate an SVP role that was redundant, at least for now. That made sense to Shirley too, and she quickly agreed to support the change in her meeting with Henry the following week.

But she didn't.

In fact, in a follow-up email that included Peter, Henry made clear that Shirley would continue reporting directly to him. Peter and Shirley passed in the hall that afternoon.

"What happened?" Peter asked Shirley.

"It was Henry's decision," replied Shirley.

And that was that.

Peter checked with Henry, who said that Shirley felt that reporting to the COO would be better for her CV in the future. But

Peter felt betrayed by Shirley. How could she do that to him? It was so selfish. She made an agreement and then just changed her mind, and now Peter felt slighted and marginalised in front of Henry.

Peter decided that he couldn't trust her anymore, and that he would make sure she knew it.

Months went by, and Shirley's betrayal of Peter and Peter's ongoing distrust of Shirley degenerated into a cold war in the operations department. The two siloed off their information from each other, criticised each other's initiatives, and avoided speaking to each other whenever possible.

Peter was so hurt by this that when he brought the story to me in our coaching session a year later, he listed it as one of the worst interpersonal relationships he had ever had at work. I asked him to let go of the idea that there was only one possible interpretation of what had happened.

I asked him to imagine instead what Shirley had done on a spectrum of various possible interpretations. On one end, Shirley hated Peter and wanted to hurt and embarrass him. On the other end, it was somehow a good move for the company that Peter simply had no understanding of or visibility on.

> I WASN'T ASKING PETER TO QUESTION WHAT HE HAD HEARD, ONLY WHAT HE UNDERSTOOD IT TO MEAN.

I wasn't asking Peter to question what he had heard, only what he understood it to mean. The facts of the case remained the same across the entire spectrum of possible meanings. But he had to admit that based on the information he had, one end of the spectrum was just as possible as the other.

"Let's try to understand Shirley for a minute, shall we?" I asked Peter. "What could the structural change have meant to her?"

"Well, she's no longer reporting to the COO, which isn't a demotion, by the way."

"True," I replied, "but if her role reporting to yours eliminates the need for an SVP of Safety permanently, then you've not only taken away the COO reporting line from her CV in the future; you've eliminated a potential promotion for her. Is it possible that she was just doing what was best for her with the resources and relationships she had available to her at the time? And wouldn't you do the same?"

I saw the lights go on behind Peter's eyes. Suddenly he saw it. Nothing of what was said, or what was heard, had changed … but what Peter understood it to mean had changed completely.

I continued. "Consider the possibility that you've misunderstood what Shirley was doing in that situation. How likely is it that she might have felt threatened by shifting her reporting line from Henry to you, even if it made sense structurally?"

"Very likely," admitted Peter.

I agreed. "It very likely wasn't malicious, or deceptive. And it had nothing at all to do with you. And now you've wasted a year of relationship alienating each other. Imagine the decisions you both could have been making better if you'd been sharing information and talking things through together. And imagine Henry's disappointment having had to referee between two team members that he trusts and counts on all this time." I was done.

Peter immediately committed to change his posture towards Shirley. He didn't feel rehashing things after so long would be beneficial, so instead he made a unilateral decision to change the nature of the relationship. Two silos in the company came crashing down that day, and the only thing that had changed in the situation was Peter's understanding of Shirley's communication.

COSTS OF FEELING MISUNDERSTOOD

Misunderstanding and other forms of conflict cost our companies in increases in absenteeism, lost productivity, increased health care costs, and often legal fees. One study found that the average employee spends 2.8 hours/week dealing with conflict.[77]

---

77 CPP. (2008). Workplace conflict and how businesses can harness it to thrive.

That's more than 145 hours every year, per employee. That's intense! And very expensive!

- **Big companies**: A study across 400 companies with more than 100,000 employees found that on average misunderstandings cost each company USD 62.4 million per year (**FP8.2**).[78]
- **Mid-sized companies**: An in-depth case study of a law firm of 300 employees found that poor communications between employees cost the company around a million dollars every year.[79]
- **Small companies**: A study of SMEs with only about 100 employees each found that they forfeit an average of USD 420,000 per year due to misunderstandings and miscommunication at work.[80]

Do you see how important it is for us to get this right? Being heard is not enough: we need to be understood, and to understand each other.

- 75% of employees don't feel understood on important topics like benefits, safety, and time-off, and

78　Grossman, D. (July 17, 2011). The cost of poor communications. *The Holmes Report.*

79　Cherniss, C., & Goleman, D. (2001). *The emotionally intelligent workplace: How to select for measure, and improve emotional intelligence in individuals, groups, and organisations.* Jossey-Bass.

80　Hamilton, D. (2010). Top ten email blunders that cost companies money. *Creative Communications & Training.*

- 40% of employees feel that even if their feedback is understood, it doesn't lead to actionable change.[81]

But wait, what if the employee is just a whiner?

WHINEY EMPLOYEES

Sometimes employees who do speak-up but don't get what they want can feel that they haven't been heard or understood. And (trust me) it can get seriously irritating for a manager who feels they've already heard and addressed an employee's concerns to keep hearing them again and again. So relationships can break down when employees whine, which often leads to fewer opportunities for the employee.

> WHEN I TALK ABOUT HELPING EMPLOYEES FEEL UNDERSTOOD, I'M TALKING ABOUT THE VAST MAJORITY WHO CURRENTLY DON'T, NOT THOSE WHO CONTINUE TO WHINE ABOUT THINGS THEY'VE BEEN HEARD ON ALREADY.

When employees overestimate the value of their voice to their manager, they tend to receive lower performance ratings and are at higher risk of termination.[82] So it's important

81 UKG. (2021). The heard and the heard-nots. Retrieved from https://workforceinstitute.org/wp-content/uploads/The-Heard-and-the-Heard-Nots.pdf.

82 Burris, E. R., Detert, J. R., & Romney, A. C. (2013). Speaking up vs. being heard: The disagreement around and outcomes of employee voice. *Organisation Science, 24*(1), 22-38.

to consider both the manager's and the employee's perspectives in the valuation of voice in the relationship.

Certainly, some employees might be just cranky and greedy, but that can't be true of the 75% of our workforce who don't feel heard (**FP8.3**).[83] When I talk about helping employees feel understood, I'm talking about the vast majority who currently don't, not those who continue to whine about subjects on which they've been heard already.

If you have a truly whiney employee who has been heard and feels understood and yet won't move on from their concern, here's what you can do:

1. Reiterate their understanding: Clearly communicate to the employee that their concerns have been understood and addressed. Make sure that they agree with you that they have been understood.
2. Set expectations: Let the employee know what can and cannot be changed in response to their concerns, and why certain decisions have been made.
3. Seek solutions: Encourage the employee to propose possible solutions to their issues. This might help them see the situation from a problem-solving perspective.

---

83   UKG. (2021). The heard and the heard-nots. Retrieved from https://workforceinstitute.org/wp-content/uploads/The-Heard-and-the-Heard-Nots.pdf.

4. Provide feedback: Communicate the impact of constant complaining on the work environment and on the employee's professional growth.
5. Involve HR or Mediation: If the situation doesn't improve, it may be necessary to involve HR or a mediator to ensure a fair and impartial handling of the situation.

MISUNDERSTANDING OR A REAL DISPUTE

Not all disagreements are simple misunderstandings, and better understanding won't resolve all disputes. In *When Talking Makes Things Worse* (1997) author David Steibel helpfully outlines three questions we can answer in order to figure out if we are facing a misunderstanding or a genuine disagreement. We should ask:

1. Can I do anything to change their mind?
2. If I listened and understood them, would they feel satisfied and stop opposing me?
3. If they explained themselves to me more, would I change my position?[84]

If the answers are all "no," then it's not a misunderstanding, it's a real dispute.

---

84 Steibel, D., (1997). *When talking makes things worse!* Whitehall & Norton.

I like Steibel's questions, but the example from Peter and Shirley makes me think he's missing one. Peter hadn't changed Shirley's mind, hadn't spent more time listening to Shirley, and he hadn't received any further explanation from Shirley. So, when Peter came to me with his story, it really was in his mind a genuine dispute. Yet Peter changed his mind, dissolved the dispute, and transformed the relationship, which leads me to suggest a fourth guiding question:

4. Have I considered all of the possible understandings available to me, and chosen the most loving one?

If the answer to the first three questions is "no" and the answer to the last question is "yes," then you've got a real dispute, not a misunderstanding. And that's okay. Disputes, like misunderstandings, aren't evil.

DEFAULT TO POSITIVITY

We always have the choice to understand each other as evil, malicious, deceitful, and manipulative if we want to, but I find very few people truly belong to those categories. Even those who have done terrible things in the past typically don't turn them into a lifestyle choice. Most people, most of the time, do what they feel works for them and what they think is right, and relatively few people ever have enough malintent towards another person to wilfully cause pain.

I think the majority of the world's population is morally good. That's a positivity default that helps me to love people I don't agree with.

It makes sense to me that if we are to seek understanding with each other, we should start from the default position of the best possible understanding that works for us. In other words, we should be giving each other the benefit of the doubt, not only because it's the loving thing to do, but also because it's often the most pragmatic.

Peter regained an otherwise lost relationship by assigning a new understanding to an old event. That gave him access to more information to do a better job and have a better life at work. Peter chose a new positive understanding of Shirley and transformed an adversary into an ally.

> YOU CAN CHOOSE WHERE YOU START WITH YOUR INTERPRETATION, SO TRY STARTING FROM THE BEST POSSIBLE UNDERSTANDING AND SEE IF IT CHANGES THE QUALITY OF YOUR LIFE AND RELATIONSHIPS.

We can all do that!

Whatever was said has been said, and whatever was done has been done. But what it means is entirely up to you, because you're the only person who experiences what something means to *you*. So when listening for understanding, try to fix that truth as the starting place for your interpretation. It's your choice – so try starting from the best possible interpretation and see if it changes the quality of your life and relationships.

FUNGUS AS FOOD: DISAGREEMENT AS UNDERSTANDING

Yes, you read that right. A conflict resulting in permanent disagreement can lead to understanding too. Just hang on.

First of all, dispute is not the same as disagreement. A dispute is an ongoing struggle. Disagreement can be a permanent state without any ongoing struggle (**FP8.4**).

On this third level of the connectedness process – climbing from Included at the bottom towards Loved at the top – it's important to recognise that being understood doesn't necessarily require agreement. Disagreement can be a quality of a loving relationship too, as long as there's understanding.

This idea can get a little touchy, so I'll give you a personal life example. Something simple.

Nicole and I don't disagree on much, but there is one sincere disagreement that remains unresolved in our relationship: mushrooms.

She loves them.

I hate them.

Let's begin …

When we first started dating, she ordered mushroom risotto for dinner one night. I snarled at her.

"How can you eat that?"

"What?"

"It's got mushrooms in it."

I refused to kiss her after dinner. The very idea of it just grossed me out. She had the nerve to suggest that mushrooms were a genuine food item [*insert eye roll here*]: "nutritious and tasty," she called them.

"Disgusting," I replied. "It's a fungus that grows in shit. Actually, shit is the only necessary ingredient in the production of poop-fungus. It doesn't belong on human plates." (**FP8.5**)

Now at this point she could have thrown her hands up at me and called the whole thing off. I'd clearly insulted not just her taste in food, but her intelligence. If it really was poop-fungus on a plate, wasn't she intelligent enough to know that for herself? But she wasn't deterred from the relationship, so she leaned into the dispute.

"Consider the possibility," she said to me, "that what occurs to you as poop-fungus might occur to me as nutritious and tasty. I hear you that you don't like them, but I'm not asking you to eat them with me, and I promise not to make any food for you with mushrooms in it."

It's been five years since that night.

> "WE'VE COME TO AN UNDERSTANDING" MEANS THAT WE HAVE AGREED TO DISAGREE, BUT THAT WHAT WE DO AGREE ON IS THAT OUR RELATIONSHIP IS MORE VALUABLE THAN OUR DISAGREEMENT.

She still eats mushrooms for dinner sometimes (gross!). When she does, she always cooks them separately from everything else, and stirs them in only on her plate, which means they're never a part of even the flavour profile of my food. And I still refuse to kiss her after she eats them, which is perhaps why she doesn't cook them all that often. She's clearly a saint in all of this, and I'm just an intolerant fool, but even though we disagree sharply on the edibility of poop-fungus, we've come to an understanding about mushrooms.

"We've come to an understanding" means that we have agreed to disagree, but that what we do agree on is that our relationship is more valuable than our disagreement (**FP8.6**).

That's where we need to get to in our organisations, and in our leadership.

It happens sometimes that even after understanding each other perfectly, parties cannot come to an agreement. I'm perfectly comfortable saying that I love someone I don't agree with; agreement isn't a pre-requisite for love, whereas understanding is (**FP8.7**).

FEELING UNDERSTOOD

Remember, for a person to feel understood, they need to feel included and heard, and then they need to hear an echo back to them that at least roughly approximates what they themselves have said. This involves active listening, a major concern for organisational leaders.

> When direct managers create safe working environments, 79% of employees feel that their perspectives matter, a measure that drops to 36% for employees whose managers do not create a safe working environment. Employees who believe their managers support them have a 4% attrition risk versus 17% for employees who feel their managers do not support them.[85]

If you're a good manager, you've probably already read what's out there on active listening. You already know how to empathise and nod your head from time to time to indicate your interest.

---

85   Baumeister, R., & Leary, M. (1995). The need to belong: Desire for interpersonal attachments as a fundamental human motivation. *Psychological Bulletin, 117*(3), 497-529.

You're not part of the 63% of managers whose employees say don't listen to them.[86] You may well be the best manager ever! So you're thinking about just flipping ahead and skipping this section.

But if you do, you'll miss something important.

Consider this: suppose you thought of yourself as a good active listener, but your people didn't experience you that way. Would you want to know? Are you open to feedback?

If you are, here's the mirror.

CARE AND CURIOSITY

My definition provides a quick test for active listening:

Active Listening = Care + Curiosity (**FP8.8**)

That's it. In my experience those are the core components in active listening. If you genuinely care about the person you are listening to, and you are genuinely curious about what they're saying and what it means to them, then just follow your instinct. You'll naturally do all of the things involved in active listening. You'll

---

86   Glint. (2021). State of the manager. Retrieved from https://www.glintinc. com/wp-content/uploads/2021/03/State_of_the_Manager_2021.pdf.

- encourage a safe environment,
- invite transparency,
- ask for clarification,
- communicate interest, and
- empathise with them in a way that makes them feel understood.

That's the whole shebang. If you have care and curiosity, you don't need to remember the rest. So internalise that for a minute, and then ask yourself:

- Do I really care about each of my employees all of the time?
- Am I always genuinely curious about what they're saying and what it means to them?

If the answer to either of those is "no" then you're going to have to move on to the mechanics of active listening. But don't worry, I'm here to help.

LISTENING FOR UNDERSTANDING – ACTIVE LISTENING

Here's the truth: although curiosity is one of my core values, care is not. People can be really irritating to me; what they're talking about can seem irrelevant. Sometimes it takes a bit of mindfulness, of being present in the moment, for me to muster up the care and empathy required for a smooth transition from tolerance to active listening, especially with people I think are boring or incompetent.

That's when I need to work at it, and active listening becomes a conscious effort.

I'm grateful for Heather R. Younger's active listening model.[87] Her model differs from mine in that she doesn't present being heard, understood, and valued as stages of a relationship, but as qualities of commnuication in an organisation. She describes active listening as taking place in five steps:

Step 1: Recognise the unsaid

Leaders need to be aware of the unvocalised and often involuntary pieces of communication that aren't being highlighted verbally in a conversation. It takes emotional intelligence to create a safe space for people to speak and to pay attantion to what's *not* being said.

ASK YOURSELF: What aren't they saying?

---

87   Younger, H. R. (2023). *The art of active listening: How people at work feel heard, valued, and understood.* Berrett-Koehler.

Step 2: Seek to understand

In this step, the input you receive as a listener needs to be disconnected from the personal filters through which you are interpretting it. Instead, it should be interpreted through your understanding of the filters of the speaker from whom you've heard it (**FP8.9**). In my experience, this is an impossible ideal. We should definitely try as much as we can to recognise our prejudices and biases, but even for trained professionals in psychology, this is a difficult challege.

ASK YOURSELF: What does what they said mean to them?

Step 3: Decode

Decoding is when you reflect on the truth of what you're hearing from the communicator. You might identify gaps in your own knowlegde that could lead to insights for you. Identifying with another person's truth is already an act of care.

ASK YOURSELF: What does what they said mean for me?

Step 4: Act

This is when you've compiled the new information into a plan of action. It's the action that shows the speaker that their voice truly matters. In a leadership relationship, these change initiatives show how much you value the input you've received.

ASK YOURSELF: What needs to be done with this?

Step 5: Close the loop

It's important to communicate back to the person or people you are listening to not only what you understood, but what you've done about it. It's important that they become aware of any changes you've made as a result, and that they have a chance to reflect on whether those changes are meaningful to them.

ASK THE OTHER PERSON: Did I get that right?

The most critical contribution Younger makes is that she highlights the need for leaders to remove themselves from the understanding process. People speak from their own positions, through their own biases, heuristics, assumptions, and world-views. And often the most challenging thing to do in active listening is to suspend your own biases, heuristics, assumptions, and worldview – so that you can truly understand the person you are listening to.

IF YOU WANT TO BE UNDERSTOOD, SEEK TO UNDERSTAND

The closer you get to another person, the more you share with them. The more you share, the more opportunity there is for misunderstanding and disagreement. And there's a lot of people with whom I both spend time *and* disagree.

One of the best principles I know for resolving misunderstandings and conflict is that both parties seeking understanding should be able to reiterate the position of the other in a way that the other person approves of it. I should be able to tell you what you are saying in a way that makes sense to you. Only then will you feel understood. But that doesn't mean we need to agree with each other to be able to move on to the next stage in our relationship.

Understanding is more valuable than agreement because being together is more important than being right.

FIRST PRINCIPLES

FP8.1 UNDERSTOOD = HEARD + ECHO

FP8.2 Misunderstandings at work cost our companies millions of dollars in lost profits.

FP8.3 Most employees don't feel that they are understood at work.

FP8.4 A dispute is an ongoing conflict; a disagreement can be a permanent state in a relationship.

FP8.5   Mushrooms are gross. ;-)

FP8.6   Understanding is more important than agreement.

FP8.7   You can love someone you disagree with.

FP8.8   Active listening is simply care and curiosity.

FP8.9   To understand the person you're listening to, you'll need to remove your filters and try to apply what you know of theirs.

NEXT STEPS

1. When someone is speaking to you, listen with care and curiosity.

2. In a dispute, consider that you have a spectrum of possible interpretations to choose from, then choose the most loving possible interpretation available to you.

3. Think of a disagreement you have with someone. Try to repeat back to them what they've said to you in a way they approve of.

EVOLUTIONARY PSYCHOLOGY OF SOCIAL INFLUENCE

CHAPTER 9

VALUED

When Insight Sparks Transformation

"NO ONE CARES HOW MUCH YOU KNOW UNTIL THEY KNOW HOW MUCH YOU CARE."

—PRESIDENT THEODORE ROOSEVELT

VALUED = UNDERSTOOD + MEANINGFUL CHANGE (FP9.1)

STARLINE WINDOWS

When I was nineteen, I got a job at the Starline Windows factory in Vancouver, Canada. I started out working on the glazing line. I would tape the inside of the welded frames, then drop sealed glass panes into them. There was a lot of us on the line, all banging away under the leadership of our line manager.

Terry was a big guy, funny, hardworking, and great with the team. My memories of that time are fading now, but I distinctly recall Terry always keeping us motivated with stories, jokes, and music. We listened to Vancouver's Rock 101 radio station, and it was not uncommon for us to all start singing along to "Dirty Deeds" or "Hard Sun."

We were a bit of a gang in that factory, constantly teasing each other, yelling at each other to get stuff done, and listening to each other's stories about what trouble we got up to on the weekends. Most Fridays, especially if we'd had a hard week, Terry and Tim (the Factory Manager) would order pizza for the guys and we would all have lunch together on the factory floor.

I don't remember the names of most of the guys I worked with each day, but I do remember having the time of my life doing it. I had an insatiable sense of curiosity, so I'd quickly get bored once I'd learned a new skill, and I'd bug Terry to move me to a new area of the plant. He'd move me to a different section of the production line, and once I'd learned it, I'd ask to be moved again.

But what was interesting is that whenever I made the request, he made the change. He didn't like moving me from a spot where I was really good, but he soon realised that it didn't take me long to become good at pretty much everything he gave me to do. So he was adding value to me by keeping me interested, and I to him by becoming more versatile.

After a few months I became a sharp tool for Tim and Terry because they could put me anywhere in the factory and I could deliver well. I welded frames, cut glass, and eventually made it to the custom line, where we would create all kinds of curved and odd-shaped windows.

When I turned my thumb into a hamburger on the table saw, Terry took me to the hospital to patch me up. And when I got a glass sliver in my eyeball (yes, that happened), it was Terry who pulled it out with tweezers. I remember sitting in front of him in the medical room, with his face an inch from mine. He told me jokes to keep me calm and kept reminding me not to blink.

Terry was more than a manager; he was a friend, a leader, a mentor, a confidant, and just a generally good man. I loved that guy, for real, though I would have never said so out loud. Guys on factory lines don't tell each other they love each other unless it's late on a Friday and we've had too many beers to know better.

I never told Tim and Terry how grateful I was, and am still, for that experience. The work we did was hard, fast, and sometimes dangerous. I still bear scars that I earned working alongside them. But I'll happily keep the scars as a reminder of what it felt like to be in that factory. I felt cared for, encouraged, developed, and empowered. And when I spoke up, they did things differently.

That's how I know they truly valued me.

EVOLUTIONARY PSYCHOLOGY OF SOCIAL INFLUENCE

Okay, that heading has a lot of big words in it, I get it. I'll make it simple.

It's possible to feel heard and understood by someone and not feel valued by them, or value them in return. You'll probably relate to this both in and outside of your work. The difference between feeling understood and feeling valued is meaningful change (**FP9.2**).

- If the person you feel understood by does something because they've been influenced by what you've said, you feel valued by them.
- If you have a change of heart, change of mind, or change of behaviour as a result of hearing and understanding someone else, it's because you value them.

For you to know that you value another person, you need to let what they say and do influence what you say and do. And for you to feel valued by another person, you need to see that what you say and do influences what they say and do.

This principle is called reciprocity, and it's a million-year-old best practise for human survival.

Think of it like this: for most of the last million years of human evolution the world has been a very scary and often inhospitable place. Scarcity and violence ruled both the natural world and the societies we humans created for tens of thousands of generations. How can you best protect yourself and make sure you are provided for when you're surrounded by a tonne of natural threats and other apex predators (i.e. other humans)?

You join a team.

We humans learned millennia ago that we are stronger together. So to survive we formed families, tribes, gangs, cities, nations, empires, religions, and more recently: companies. Maybe that's why, after 10,000 generations of figuring out who to trust, finding friends is the core function of about 80% of our brain's makeup.[88]

- But how do we know who's on our team?
- Who can we trust to provide for us and protect us?
- Who should we work with, and how should we behave in that relationship, organisation, or society?
- Who should we allow to influence us, and who should we try to influence?

Well, it depends on the goal we have in mind.

If our goal is to find a romantic partner, the people we allow to influence us will not be the same as if we were trying to make

---

88   Baumeister, R., & Leary, M. (1995). The need to belong: Desire for interpersonal attachments as a fundamental human motivation. *Psychological Bulletin, 117*(3), 497-529.

more money, raise our kids, survive cancer, or protect ourselves during a physical attack. Different domains require different influencers. In the broadest sense, there are six evolutionary domains in which people pursue goals and seek influencers:

1. Protecting / providing for ourselves,
2. Having a supportive social environment,
3. Finding a partner,
4. Protecting our partner,
5. Raising our kids,
6. Establishing our status in society.[89]

Those are the big contexts in which humans tend to pursue goals (**FP9.3**). And who we allow to influence us is different in each of those goal domains. We figure out who our influencers are based on six major principles of influence:

1. Reciprocity – people respond in-kind to people who have helped them in some way in the past.
2. Liking – people do things for other people they like.
3. Scarcity – people do something because it's scarce or fleeting (i.e. FOMO: Fear of Missing Out).
4. Social proof – people are influenced by someone because other people have been influenced by the same person.

---

89   Sundie, J.M., Cialdini, R.B., Griskevicius, V. & Kenrick, D.T. (2012). The world's (truly) oldest profession: Social influence in evolutionary perspective, *Social Influence, 7*(3), 134-153. See also Koerner, A. F., & Floyd, K. (2010). Evolutionary perspectives on interpersonal relationships. *New directions in interpersonal communication research, 27-47.*

5. Authority – people are influenced by another person's power or expertise.
6. Commitment and Consistency – people do what they said they would do and what they've committed to do.[90]

There are one or more goal-based influencers behind pretty much every decision you've ever made your whole life (**FP9.4**). That's because you are a complex social being, and figuring out who should influence you is what helped all of your ancestors survive.

THE BOSS AS INFLUENCER

Let's quickly recap: we know we value someone when we change our mind, heart, and/or behaviours following something that person has said or done, based on a combination of our own goals and who they are (among the six principles of influence above).

Now let's put this in a work context, with our boss as the influencer.

Your goals at work aren't really based on your KPI's, are they? Let's be honest. You're probably not there because you're deeply committed to Excel spreadsheets, graphic design, the

---

90   Sundie, J. M., Cialdini, R. B., Griskevicius, V., & Kenrick, D. T. (2006). Evolutionary social influence. In M. Schaller, J. A. Simpson, & D. T. Kenrick (Eds.), *Evolution and social psychology* (pp. 287-316). Psychosocial Press.

movement of tyres around the world, or the art of making fancy coffee. You're most likely there because of one or more of the six goal domains above. You want to survive, take care of your family, and live well in society.

> **YOUR GOALS AT WORK AREN'T REALLY BASED ON YOUR KPI'S, ARE THEY? LET'S BE HONEST.**

Being there provides for you and protects you as a part of a supportive social environment in the workplace. The money you gain from being there helps you in your relationships outside of work and contributes to raising your kids (if you have any); it gives you social status so that you (and others) know that you are a valued member of society.

Your boss likely has some direct or indirect influence on all of these goal-domains in your life, but how much influence will be based on where your boss sits among the influencer principles. Your boss might call you into their office and tell you to do something, and you can hear and understand them, but whether you value them or not will be based on who they are *to you*:

1. Have they helped you in some way in the past? (Reciprocity)
2. Do you like them as a person? (Liking)
3. Do they want to include you in something? (Scarcity)
4. Do other people you trust also trust them? (Social proof)
5. Are they competent? Or, do they have power over you? (Authority)

6. Did you make a deal with them to do what they're asking you to do? (Commitment and consistency)

The more questions you can answer "yes" to, the more you will value what your boss is telling you – and the more likely you are to allow what they're saying change your heart, your mind, and your behaviour, and be happy about it.

We call "engaged" the employee who is readily influenced (to do what they believe is going to help them achieve their goals) by leaders who meet most or all of those criteria. Employee engagement is the by-product of an employee seeing their relationship with their organisation and boss as mutually beneficial.

ORGANISATIONAL BENEFITS OF EMPLOYEES WHO FEEL VALUED

The most widespread and in-depth studies of employee engagement in recent years have been conducted by Gallup. In one such study, across 50,000 business units covering 47 industries and 20 years of data (including 1.4 million employees), higher employee engagement was shown to result in an average of:

- 41% less absenteeism,
- Between 24% and 59% less turnover,
- 70% fewer safety incidents,
- 40% fewer defects,
- 10% higher customer ratings,

- 17% higher productivity,
- 20% higher sales, and
- 21% higher profitability (**FP9.5**).[91]

Gallup's definition of employee engagement is comprised of several elements, including an employee's sense of purpose and self-development, a concentration on their strengths rather than weaknesses, and recognition that their job isn't just a job, but half of their life every day. These qualities are in line with goal-pursuit in the areas of self-protection, social status, and finding a supportive social environment.

IT'S THE MANAGER

But more important than all of these is the employee's relationship with their direct line manager. Employees prefer an ongoing conversation in a coaching-style relationship with their manager to periodical performance reviews in a boss-subordinate relationship. The manager-employee relationship accounts for 70% of the variance in all of the organisational benefits of employee engagement mentioned above (**FP9.6**).[92]

And what were those conditions again?

1. Coaching style of leadership, and

---

91   Harter, C.J.J. (2019). *It's the Manager*. Gallup Press.
92   Ibid.

2. Ongoing conversations.

These conditions are established by the principles of influence (reciprocity, liking, scarcity, social proof, authority, commitment and consistency) and they are the natural ingredients in what I describe as being valued at work. But they're also what great leaders themselves are saying is great leadership.

In 2019, all of the nominees for the Gallup Manager of the Year Award were gathered for a round table discussion on leadership. They were asked about how they lead, navigate change, and develop their teams, and this is what they said:

1. Connect company purpose to individual and team action.
2. Shine a light on the opinions of others and make them count.
3. Coach your team in a way that allows for genuine candour.
4. Commit to one meaningful conversation a week with each team member.
5. Unlock human motivation by connecting work to a person's innate tendencies.
6. Recognise and reward excellence.
7. Care about your employees as real people.
8. Make your No. 1 job the development of new stars.[93]

Have a quick look at these behaviours: are any of them possible outside of the six principles of influence?

---

93   Gallup. (2019). 8 behaviours of the world's best managers. Retrieved from https://www.gallup.com/workplace/272681/habits-world-best-managers.aspx.

No. Way.

These leaders are telling us that their keys to managerial success don't stop with them helping their team members to feel heard and understood. The best managers in the world know from experience that if you want people to perform at their natural best under your leadership, they have to want to follow you. That will only happen if you add value to their lives and acknowledge the value that they add to yours.

> **IF YOU WANT PEOPLE TO PERFORM AT THEIR NATURAL BEST UNDER YOUR LEADERSHIP, THEY HAVE TO WANT TO FOLLOW YOU. THAT WILL ONLY HAPPEN IF YOU ADD VALUE TO THEIR LIVES AND ACKNOWLEDGE THE VALUE THAT THEY ADD TO YOURS.**

LISTENING TO VALUE OTHERS

If you want someone to value your voice in a way that influences their thoughts and behaviours, you should probably start by listening to their voice first. I'm a firm believer that every person is the expert on their own unique blend of knowledge and experience, which means I can learn from anyone. Good leaders know this. Do you recall from the last chapter that the core ingredients in listening for understanding are care and curiosity?

Good, now let's add learning.

ACTIVE LISTENING FOR VALUE = CARE + CURIOSITY + LEARNING

If I'm listening to you with curiosity and care, I'm actively listening. I'm listening to understand you. But in addition to curiosity and care, I can also listen with the intent to learn something from you. If I do, what you'll say might change my heart, my mind, or my behaviour in some way, and you will feel valued in our relationship (**FP9.7**).

Think about it this way: how do we communicate value?

We change.

If someone gives us advice and we change our behaviour as a result, then it was valuable advice. If we understand the advice but don't change, it wasn't. This is why so many managers are so bad with feedback, because even if they listen with curiosity and care to their employees' feedback, they often don't listen with the intent to learn from it. So the employee often ends up feeling understood but devalued.

They say things like, "Well, I told him, but he never does anything about it, so why bother?"

It's change that communicates the value of feedback, not understanding. Understanding is just a step along the way.

IF YOU WANT TO FEEL VALUED, VALUE OTHERS

This is the most overlooked of obvious pieces of advice. You've probably heard the quote attributed to Mahatma Gandhi: "Be the change you want to see in the world." But that wasn't what he said. It's a paraphrase; what he actually said was WAY better:

> We but mirror the world. All the tendencies present in the outer world are to be found in the world of our body. If we could change ourselves, the tendencies in the world would also change. As a man changes his own nature, so does the attitude of the world change towards him. This is the divine mystery supreme. A wonderful thing it is and the source of our happiness. We need not wait to see what others do.[94]

I was fortunate enough to learn this lesson in my early twenties. If you want people to add value to you, add so much value to them that it's impossible for them not to respond. I've kept that in mind throughout my career, and I try to lead by adding value and valuing others. When I allow them to change me, they feel valued. And when they change because of me, I feel valued too.

We are a social species, and we naturally gravitate to people who add value to our lives, and to whose lives we add value.

---

94 Ranseth, J. (2015). Gandhi didn't actually ever say "Be the change you want to see in the world." Here's the real quote. Retrieved from https://josephranseth. com/gandhi-didnt-say-be-the-change-you-want-to-see-in-the-world/.

And what if we are able to consistently add value to each other in a relationship that improves the quality of each other's lives? You guessed it, it must be love.

But we still have to address the implications of sex and romance in the workplace if we're going to develop a real expression of love at work, and perhaps a model for loving leadership. So next we'll look at workplace relationships where sex is rumoured to be happening but isn't (real love), and we'll discuss the potential for sexual tension in close relationships in the workplace (not real love).

FIRST PRINCIPLES

FP9.1   VALUED = UNDERSTOOD + MEANINGFUL CHANGE

FP9.2   People feel valued when what they communicate leads to meaningful change.

FP9.3   People most often choose goals based on survival, partnering, parenting, and having a good standing in society.

FP9.4   People allow others to influence them based on Reciprocity, Liking, Scarcity, Social proof, Authority, and Commitment / Consistency.

FP9.5   Companies whose employees feel valued have:
- 41% less absenteeism,
- Between 24% and 59% less turnover,
- 21% higher profitability.

FP9.6 Seventy per cent of the variance on those benefits comes down to the relationship between an employee and their line manager.

FP9.7 Active listening for value involves care, curiosity, and listening for learning.

NEXT STEPS

1. When your employees are speaking to you, listen with care and curiosity, but also with the intent to learn from them and apply what you are learning.
2. If you haven't already, change your management style to a coaching style.
3. Make sure you are having ongoing conversations with all your teammates at work, not just periodical performance reviews.
4. Consider: what will you change about yourself and your leadership style as a result of what you've understood from this chapter?

PART THREE

RUNNING INTO
LOVE AT WORK

Ch. 12: Loving Leadership

Ch. 11: Kinds of Unlove

Ch. 10: Something to Talk
About

Part 3: Running into Love at Work

ME AND MY SPOUCE'S SPOUCES

CHAPTER 10

SOMETHING TO TALK ABOUT

Sex, Romance, and the Work-Spouse

"I BELIEVE THAT PEOPLE ARE CONNECTED AT THE HEART, AND IT DOESN'T MATTER WHAT YOU DO, OR WHO YOU ARE, OR WHERE YOU LIVE, THERE ARE NO BOUNDARIES OR BARRIERS IF TWO PEOPLE ARE MEANT TO BE TOGETHER."

—JULIA ROBERTS

ME AND MY SPOUSE'S SPOUSES

In spite of the potential for confusion, love is already present at work. The word "love" isn't entirely foreign vocabulary in the office.

I've heard employees say, "I absolutely love my boss," to indicate that they feel supported and empowered in their role. And I've heard managers say, "I love my team," to express genuine appreciation for the sense of community they experience at work. I've witnessed an employee rushing to throw a last-minute document on his manager's desk being greeted with, "Oh! Are those the numbers? I love you, man. I needed that. That's great!" I've also heard my wife say of one of her direct reports, "I love Alice. No, really. I genuinely love her. She's definitely my work-spouse."

The work-spouse phenomenon is not new, and it's definitely a love-at-work thing.

Dianna was my first work-spouse. I hired her as my Executive Assistant when I was building an educational organisation in the late 1990's and we grew large enough that I couldn't manage the administration anymore. Dianna and I spent a lot of time together. In fact, I spent more time with her during those years than I did with my first wife, especially after the birth of our first child.

I was working a lot and at home a lot less.

Dianna and I not only worked together; we often travelled together, ate together, spent late nights working on projects together. In that kind of environment, one where we shared a lot of life and believed strongly in the work we were doing together, it was inevitable that we became very close friends.

Now, I can hear your concern about the potential romantic evolution of our relationship, but it actually never once strayed into any gestures of romance. Although she was an attractive young woman, and I a not-so-bad looking young man, I never registered any sexual tension between us. We remained strictly platonic, and yet intimately connected through our shared life at work. I trusted her completely, and she trusted me too.

She was my work-spouse.

ARE CLOSE WORKPLACE FRIENDSHIPS A GOOD THING?

Work-spouses exist where there is love in the workplace. The work-spouse phenomenon is now well researched; it's been described as "a special, platonic friendship with a work colleague characterised by a close emotional bond, high levels of disclosure and support, and mutual trust, honesty, loyalty, and respect."[95] It has also been called a working relationship that is "modelled on a marriage relationship, with partners providing support for each other for both work and non-work related issues."[96] The work-spouse relationship forms independently of employee nationality, sexuality, or current relationship status.[97]

---

95 McBride, M.C. & Bergen K.M. (2015) Work spouses: Defining and understanding a "new" relationship. *Communication Studies, 66*(5), 487-508.

96 Vandewal. (2007). Work spouse. Retrieved from http://everything2.com/index.pl?node_id=1878594/.

97 Thorson, A. R., & McBride, M. C. (2020). Self-monitoring and other non-indicators of developing a work-spouse relationship: Implications for affective organisational commitment. *International Journal of Business Communication, 60*(3), 1000–1020.

We know the boundary between personal and professional life doesn't really exist, because work-spouse relationships are a thing. The concept of work-life balance tempts us to think that the separation of personal and professional relationships is good for us, but this is clearly not the case.

> **WE KNOW THE BOUNDARY BETWEEN PERSONAL AND PROFESSIONAL LIFE DOESN'T REALLY EXIST, BECAUSE WORK-SPOUSE RELATIONSHIPS ARE A THING.**

Work-spouses provide evidence that professional distance is often inefficient, and that work-life balance is a myth.

Buzzanell and Dohrman (2009) note that from a workplace productivity perspective, close personal relationships have often been thought to decrease performance, though they agree that it's the long hours of work and the proximity of co-workers that provide the conditions allowing close personal relationships to form.[98] Our workplace conditions definitely contribute to the formation of close relationships, that's true, but I completely disagree that close personal relationships have a negative effect on performance. That's not true at all.

Firstly, we can't place people who work well together and communicate clearly next to each other for 200 hours every month and expect them not to get close emotionally. We're social

---

98 Buzzanell, P. M., & Dohrman, R. L. (2009). Supervisors, subordinates, and coworkers. In W. F. Eadie (Ed.), *21st century communication: A reference handbook*. Sage.

animals, and our million years of survival and adaptation have turned us into reciprocal helping machines. Our employees share a good deal of life with each other every day, and that's what social animals do together in professional cages: they get close. It's natural and inevitable.

Secondly, we've known for a long time in the management sciences that stronger workplace friendships result in increased job satisfaction;[99] we also know this has a strong impact on profitability indicators such as job performance and talent retention.[100] And in spite of all attempts to promote ideologies like professional distance and work-life balance, the countermovement of friendship-at-work is winning. A 2018 Gallup study found that employees who said they had a "best friend" at work were more than twice as likely to feel engaged in their roles; they had a stronger sense of personal wellbeing and produced higher quality work than those who didn't (**FP10.1**).[101]

In fact, research shows that if a company with only 20% of its employees having a best friend at work could move that number

---

99 Winstead, B. A., Derlega, V. J., Montgomery, M. J., & Pilkington, C. (1995). The quality of friendships at work and job satisfaction. *Journal of Social and Personal Relationships, 12*(2), 199-215.

100 Sias, P. M. (2009). *Organising relationships: Traditional and emerging perspectives on workplace relationships.* Sage.

101 Mann, A. (2018). Why we need best friends at work. Retrieved from https://www.gallup.com/workplace/236213/why-need-best-friends-work.aspx.

up to 60%, it would benefit from 36% fewer safety incidents, 7% more customer engagement, and 12% higher profit.[102]

Yes, close workplace relationships are a good thing, both for the employees and for the company. But if encouraging love at work is a profitable best practise, then why is love at work an almost totally avoided subject?!

BRINGING LOVE BACK TO THE DISCUSSION

Let's look again at the way McBride and Bergen (2015) describe the work-spouse relationship: it's a "special, platonic friendship with a work colleague characterised by a close emotional bond, high levels of disclosure and support, and mutual trust, honesty, loyalty, and respect." They never once use the word "love" to describe this amazing human bond. I think that's odd (**FP10.2**).

But what I find more shocking is that out of the 269 workspouses in their study, not a single one of them indicated "love" as a characteristic or quality of their work-spouse relationship when they were asked to describe it in an open-ended survey.[103] It just doesn't seem plausible to me that none of the respondents used the term "love" either.

---

102 Ibid.
103 McBride, M.C. & Bergen K.M. (2015) Work spouses: Defining and understanding a "new" relationship. *Communication Studies*, 66(5), 487-508.

Of course, that study was back in 2015, and things have started changing. I'll show you.

It took another five years, but a 2020 study finally highlighted a few occurrences of the word "love" in their interviews with work-spouses. In one such example, an employee named Linda called out her work-spouse on behaviours that might be self-damaging, saying,

> At one point she [my work spouse] was directing the [department's] basic course, and frankly she wasn't doing well at it. I said to her. "This is hurting your career. You need to stop it. I love you, but you're not good at this. Let's move on."[104]

Under normal circumstances it might be devastating for one employee to tell another that they weren't good at something and were actively hurting their career. It might just be considered as unprofessional as telling them, "I love you." Yet both possibilities exist in the work-spouse relationship, where brutal honesty and love are both professional norms (**FP10.3**).

The reason one employee can say, "You suck at this" to another employee and get away with it is precisely because of the depth of trust and transparency already present in the kind of

---

104 McBride, M.C., Thorson, A.R. & Bergen K.M. (2020). An examination of individually performed and (co) managed facework: Unique communication within the work-spouse relationship. *Communication Studies,* 71(4), 489-510 (p. 498), emphasis theirs.

> IT MAY ONLY BE LOVE THAT MAKES IT POSSIBLE FOR ONE COLLEAGUE TO PROVIDE THE KIND OF FEEDBACK TO ANOTHER THAT NOT ONLY SAVES FACE, BUT RESULTS IN MEANINGFUL BEHAVIOUR CHANGE.

relationship where they might say, "I love you" to each other. It may only be love that makes it possible for one colleague to provide the kind of feedback that not only saves face, but results in meaningful behaviour change.

So why, again, have we been so deeply allergic to the word love in the workplace?

Oh, right. Sex.

Just like the high-school kids.

Okay, let's look at the state of sex in the workplace.

LOVE AND SEX AT WORK ARE ON THE RISE

Please forgive the heteronormativity in this section; I'm not trying to be exclusionary. There is a lot of data about male-female workplace relationships to review, but almost no research has been done on workplace romances within the LGBTQ+ community.

Roger Harrison (2008) was one of those brave enough to explore the topic of love at work more than a decade ago. He suggested that the reason we avoided it was because [w]e experience the same fear of [love] that we did with sex and power. Love has its wild aspects, and perhaps that is one reason we are wary of it. However, we shall not get rid of love by ignoring its operation in organisations, any more than we can avoid power or sex by denying their presence.[105]

I agree with Harrison that love can be problematic, like power and sex. And I also agree that love is already present in our organisations, at least as much as power. If power in organisations is studied, then love deserves to be observed, acknowledged, and studied too.

By saying that we should bring more love into the workplace, I'm not implying that it is absent. I'm suggesting that we make better use of what's already there. And for that we need a definition of love at work that isn't combined with

> LOVE IS ALREADY PRESENT IN OUR ORGANISATIONS, AT LEAST AS MUCH AS POWER. IF POWER IN ORGANISATIONS IS STUDIED, THEN LOVE DESERVES TO BE OBSERVED, ACKNOWLEDGED, AND STUDIED TOO.

perceptions of sex and romance. But we can't completely ignore sex and romance, because they're in the workplace too.

---

105 Harrison, R. (2008). Accessing the power of love in the workplace. Unpublished Manuscript. Freeland, WA. (p. 2). Retrieved from https://bschool.pepperdine.edu/masters-degree/organization-development/content/poweroflove.pdf.

People commonly assume that men and women can't be close friends without experiencing sexual tension. So male-female friendships at work often become sources of gossip and rumour. But what if the commonly held belief isn't scientifically true?

In fact, only 10% of females and 20% of males in close cross-sex friendships with a "significant other" report any sexual tension at all (**FP10.4**).[106] Yet the fear of perceived sexual tension is so strong that 75% of men say they think about sexual harassment issues when interacting with female colleagues. The men are being careful, and the women know it, because 66% of women say they've noticed that men seem inhibited in their interactions with women at work.[107]

We're living in fear of a rumour that isn't actually true.

Eighty per cent of people say that it's easier for them to make friends at work than outside of work,[108] and with organisations increasingly pursuing gender balance in the workplace, close friendships are increasingly occurring between male and female employees. Cross-sex work-spouse relationships will continue

---

106 Monsour, M., Harris, B., Kurzwell, N., & Beard, C. (1994). Challenges confronting cross-sex friendships: "Much ado about nothing?" *Sex Roles, 37*, 825-845.

107 Elsesser, K., & Peplau, L. A. (2006). The glass partition: Obstacles to cross-sex friendships at work. *Human Relations, 59*(8), 1077-1100. Retrieved from https://www.proquest.com/scholarly-journals/glass-partition-obstacles-cross-sex-friendships/docview/231455579/se-2.

108 Ibid.

to be one of the natural by-products of gender diversity and employees spending more time together at work.[109]

So what do we do?

We're just going to have to grow up, I guess.

If our organisations are pursuing gender balance, then we should expect increases in male/female relationships of all kinds, not just work-spouses. Well, that's exactly what we're seeing.

- The number of employees who report having had a romantic or sexual relationship with a co-worker has gone up from 58% in 2021 to 77% in 2022.
- Only 24% of employees reported having a work-spouse relationship in 2021, but that number more than doubled to 64% in 2022.[110]

In spite of decades of efforts aimed at separating the genders – through professional distance policies, rumours about sexual tension, and work-life balance ideologies – men and women at work are getting closer to each other and interacting more. It

---

109 Kirby, E. L., Wieland, S., & McBride, M. C. (2013). Work-life communication. In J. G. Oetzel & S. Ting-Toomey (Eds.), *The Sage handbook of conflict communication: Integrating theory, research, and practice* (2nd ed., pp. 377-402). Sage.

110 The Shift Work Shop. (2022). 2022 state of sexual harassment study. Accessed from https://www.theshiftworkshop.com/2022studyaccess.

seems all of us are increasingly pursuing meaningful relation-ships at work, both platonic and romantic.

But that's what happens when you put people who like each other and trust one another in close proximity for thousands of hours.

The positive aspects are great – platonic and romantic rela-tionships are both on the rise – but what about the negative aspects? Workplace romances as acts of infidelity can lead to painful experiences like divorce or family break up, and of course the workplace couple that breaks up romantically yet must continue to work together could bring some tension into the workplace. Perhaps the most obvious and measurable nega-tive impact in the workplace would be this: with more men and women working together closely and pursuing deeper rela-tionships with each other at work, we might expect to see an increase in sexual harassment as a by-product, right?

Seems reasonable … but that's not what we're seeing in the research.

SEXUAL HARASSMENT AT WORK IS IN DECLINE

There was a major spike in 2018 in the number of workplace sexual harassment claims filed with the US Equal Employment Opportunity Commission (EEOC) in the wake of the #MeToo movement.[111] More women felt more comfortable to speak out about their experiences of sexual harassment, so the spike in cases is what we might expect. But what was surprising is what happened next.

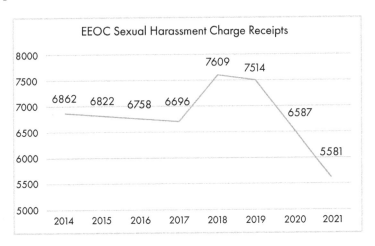

FIGURE 8:   THE DECLINE OF SEXUAL HARASSMENT COMPLAINTS IN THE US

Four years of steady decline.

In spite of significant increases in gender balance, more work-spouse relationships, and more co-workers actually having sex with each other … workplace sexual harassment declined 27% from 2018-2021 (**FP10.5**).[112]

I initially suspected that the pandemic might have had something to do with it, but remote workers are roughly 10% more

---

111   U.S. EEOC, Integrated Mission System, Charge Data, FY 2014 – FY 2021.
112   Ibid.

likely (not less) to experience workplace sexual harassment.[113] These numbers should have gone up, but they didn't.

I'm really encouraged that they've gone down.

The good news is that we are all seeking a more loving workplace. Close workplace friendships have a positive effect on job performance, employee engagement, and talent retention. And it seems that the 10% of women and 20% of men who detect sexual tension are getting better at managing themselves without crossing lines or offending each other.

Ultimately, close friendships at work are on the rise, and that's good for business.

REFRAMING LOVE AT WORK

Work-spouse relationships provide the deepest form of belonging and reciprocity known to exist between employees outside of a long-term committed romantic relationship. It's a platonic relationship characterised by a close emotional bond that includes mutual trust and support, honesty, loyalty, respect … and love.

---

113 The Shift Work Shop. (2022). 2022 state of sexual harassment study. Accessed from https://www.theshiftworkshop.com/2022studyaccess.

And although gender diversity, work-spouse relationships, and even sex at work are all on the rise, sexual harassment is in decline. We're getting better at the transparency and trust required to build all kinds of loving relationships at work: both platonic and romantic (Also see Appendix B: Flirting@Work). We want close relationships at work. They're good for employee wellbeing, and they're good for business.

The office gossips who spread sexual-tension rumours about every male/female friendship at work will become quickly overwhelmed as work-spouse relationships continue to normalise. Increasing gender balance will result in there being too many relationships to follow and talk about. Eventually the gossips will be forced to abandon the idea that all cross-sex relationships, even among work-spouses, even those characterised by "love," are influenced by sexual attraction.

After exploring definitions of love, and the growth of love in the workplace (both romantic and platonic), we will now briefly look at the opposite of love in the workplace. Learning about unlove will help us to identify the things we should be avoiding and changing if we want to make our organisations into more loving places to work.

FIRST PRINCIPLES

FP10.1 Close relationships between employees at work are good for employee wellbeing and good for business.

FP10.2 Work-spouse relationships are on the rise; they are characterised by a close emotional bond that includes mutual trust and support, honesty, loyalty, respect … and love.

FP10.3 The intimacy in a work-spouse relationship also makes possible the highest quality of critical feedback when necessary.

FP10.4 Cross-sex relationships rarely experience any sexual tension.

FP10.5 Sex between co-workers is on the rise, but sexual harassment is in decline.

NEXT STEPS

1. Who is your work-spouse? If you don't have one, then who would you say is your closest friend at work?

2. Identify five things that you can do as a leader to encourage close friendships between employees at work.

3. Review and strengthen your gender diversity policy.

CANCEL CULTURE: ATTACK AS UNLOVE

CHAPTER 11

KINDS OF UNLOVE

Attack and Withdrawal as Forms of Violence

"LET GO OF YOUR HATE."

—LUKE SKYWALKER, *STAR WARS*

CANCEL CULTURE: ATTACK AS UNLOVE

What would it feel like to feel loved and included, and then suddenly feel unloved, devalued, misunderstood, unheard, and excluded? That's a sharp fall for any human, from the peak of human connectedness to the dark sub-floors of social isolation and loneliness below the baseline of inclusion.

You may know Kevin Hart as an actor and a comedian, but he is also a savvy investor and the owner of HartBeat, a US 100-million dollar media company. In the fall of 2018, Kevin Hart publicly stepped down as the host of the 2019 Oscar Awards ceremony following public pressure and outrage over a series of tweets he had posted between 2009 and 2011. The content of the tweets was controversial even at the time. He made fun of gay people, and lamented over what he would do if he found out his own son was gay. He defended the tweets as funny.

By the time of his 2015 *Rolling Stone* article, however, he had changed his mind. The world had changed, and he recognised his need to change with it saying, "I wouldn't tell that joke today, because when I said it, the times weren't as sensitive as they are now."[114]

But all was not forgiven.

Three years later came the announcement that Hart was to host the 2019 Oscars. Within hours the internet was flooded with reposts of his 2009 tweets, along with demands for an apology. On December 6th, 2018, he posted a video refusing to apologise. But the very next day he officially stepped down, posting, "I sincerely apologise to the LGBTQ community for my insensitive words from my past."[115]

A month later Hart repeated his apology on his radio show *Straight from the Hart*, saying, "I apologise. Now we're in a space where I'm around people of the LGBTQ community, and I'm now aware of how these words make them feel, and why they say 'That shit hurt because of what I've been through' … I'm

---

114 Daw, Stephen. (2020). A complete timeline of Kevin Hart's Oscar-hosting controversy, from tweets to apologies. *Billboard Media*. https://www.billboard.com/music/awards/kevin-hart-oscar-hosting-controversy-timeline-8492982/.
115 Ibid.

riding with you guys. I understand you."[116] But it was too late, Hart had already been cancelled.

Cancel culture has been defined as "the public shaming of a target on social media, carried out or supported by a group of people, which aims to hold the target accountable for socially incorrect or unacceptable behaviour,"[117] or "a collective of typically marginalised voices 'calling out' and emphatically expressing their censure of a powerful figure."[118] Yes, what Kevin Hart experienced was certainly cancel culture.

But what of Hart's own exclusionary jokes? With his own powerful voice he had said that he was okay with expressions of violence towards members of a marginalised community. He defended violence and called it funny.

Whether what Hart said was wrong or not isn't my concern here, this isn't a book about justice. It's a book about love, and what Hart said was unloving. And what the LGBTQ+ community did in response was unloving as well. If you have strong feelings either way about this particular case, I'll humbly ask you to set aside your judgement and look only at the communication used instead.

---

116 Ibid.
117 Tandoc, E. C., Tan Hui Ru, B., Lee Huei, G., Min Qi Charlyn, N., Chua, R. A., & Goh, Z. H. (2022). #CancelCulture: Examining definitions and motivations. *New Media & Society, 0*(0).
118 Ng, E. (2020). No grand pronouncements here: Reflections on cancel culture and digital media participation. *Television & New Media 21*(6): 621-627.

Some dismiss cancel culture as just online backlash.[119] Others say it's a group formed specifically in the interest of perceived social justice.[120]

I say it's a collective expression of unlove (**FP11.1**).

And this is where it gets tricky, because love and justice are sometimes opposed. Sometimes in human societies, highlighting an injustice has only been possible through collective exclusionary action.

> **SOMETIMES IN HUMAN SOCIETIES, HIGHLIGHTING AN INJUSTICE HAS ONLY BEEN POSSIBLE THROUGH COLLECTIVE EXCLUSIONARY ACTION.**

The cases of Harvey Weinstein and Bill Cosby spring to mind. Both involved a rapid online response to repeated allegations of sexual assault by the women who trusted these men, resulting in the #metoo movement in 2017. In these cases, and many more like them, a collective expression of unlove towards criminal perpetrators is appropriate in a society that values and protects its women. It is in fact an expression of solidarity with the victims of these crimes.

---

119 Manavis, S. (July 16, 2020) "Cancel culture" does not exist,. Available at: https://www.newstatesman.com/science-tech/2020/07/cancel-culture-does-not-exist (accessed 31 March 2023).

120 Romano, A. (December 30, 2020). Why we can't stop fighting about cancel culture. Available at: https://www.vox.com/culture/2019/12/30/20879720/what-is-cancel-culture-explainedhistory-debate (accessed 31 March 2023).

But Kevin Hart committed no crime, no matter what you may think about his tweets. Hart had not trespassed on the individual rights and freedoms of any person. There was no rape, no theft, no misdemeanour to point to, and whether you agree with his views in 2009 or not, they were a legal expression of free speech, as were the backlash tweets in 2018 that led to his withdrawal from the Oscars.

So, my original question above was: what would it feel like to feel loved and included, and then to suddenly feel unloved and excluded?

Well, in 2009 you could ask any one of Hart's fans who happened to be gay, and then in 2018 you could ask Hart himself. Again, setting aside your view of justice can be challenging, but to assess the results of unloving communication in this case, that's exactly what I'm asking you to do.

It's an unfortunately common truth that hurt people hurt people. Hart's original tweet was a kind of attack, but so was the cancel culture that followed in retribution. All forms of attack, whether physical or verbal, passive or direct, digital or IRL, are forms of violence.

The road to exclusion and social isolation is paved with two kinds of violence: attack and withdrawal (**FP11.2**).

GHOSTING: WITHDRAWAL AS UNLOVE

I tell all my coachees that I don't rent my time, I rent space in my head. That's because I think about them all the time, not just when we're together. I care deeply about my coachees, and so I often try to solve their problems while I'm running, dreaming, or listening to music, none of which are traditionally "billable hours." My coachees live in my head and heart with me, so they know they're not just investing in getting access to me for an hour from time to time, they're getting access to all of me all the time, including the 80,000 hours of my life that came before the hours we spend together.

I coached Melanie for a six-month fixed term, for which I agreed that she could pay me on completion. During our last coaching session she expressed how grateful she was for the time I had invested in her. We reviewed the goals she had achieved and hugged goodbye. She said, "I owe you money," and asked if it would be okay to pay me in instalments. I agreed, and asked her only to let me know what those instalments would be so that we had shared expectations.

After I didn't hear from her for two weeks, I reached out to her.

Another week went by. I reached out again, wondering what had happened to her.

In the months that we'd worked together she was always very chatty and responsive with me. But now no response. Then suddenly, a full two months later, I got a short message indicating that she was going through something personal and would get back to me.

But what did "something personal" mean? And when would she get back to me? After all, she still hadn't indicated any plan to pay what she owed me.

I sent a nice message here and there to Melanie over the next two months but received no response. I sent emails that received no reply. I even tried to call a couple of times, but my calls were declined.

I was confused, hurt, and starting to get frustrated. I tried to give her the benefit of the doubt, but increasingly felt deceived, manipulated, and taken advantage of in our relationship. If she didn't have the means to pay, she could have let me know. If she needed more time, she could have asked. If her good intentions were truly thwarted by a personal issue that prevented her from paying, I'm certain I could have understood and maybe even helped her. But I didn't know if any of these conditions were true, because we no longer had a relationship.

Ghosting someone is not an acceptable form of communication. It is an act of violence.

Melanie withdrew from relationship with me, and in doing so stole resources from me and my family. She'd stolen time from my life that I would never get back, and she'd stolen learning

> **GHOSTING SOMEONE IS NOT AN ACCEPTABLE FORM OF COMMUNICATION. IT IS AN ACT OF VIOLENCE.**

from my education and experience that she hadn't earned.

Four months was not an acceptable amount of time to ignore a friend or colleague, much less a coach with whom you have a business agreement. Being ghosted was one of the most unloving experiences I've ever had in business (**FP11.3**). I felt personally betrayed.

What does a loving leader do when ghosted?

Well, love calls us as leaders to peacefully confront both forms of violence: attack and withdrawal. I thought about both.

Withdrawal wouldn't work since she owed me money, so I considered my counterattack. I knew the industry Melanie was in very well, and in my darkest thoughts I considered how easy it would be to crush her name in the market to teach her a lesson. Stealing from me could result in a catastrophic loss of income for her and her family. But the problem with my revenge fantasy was that I would have to be the main character, and that's not who I am.

And that's not what love does.

The loving response to violence isn't to attack back, or to withdraw further. Love confronts both attack and withdrawal with truth, and openness to reconciliation.

I asked a mutual friend to mediate, and she agreed. I then sent Melanie an email documenting the truth of our exchanges and the value that she owed me, and added that I would invite the courts into our relationship if it was necessary in order for us to reconcile.

> **THE LOVING RESPONSE TO VIOLENCE ISN'T TO ATTACK BACK, OR TO WITHDRAW FURTHER. LOVE CONFRONTS BOTH ATTACK AND WITHDRAWAL WITH THE TRUTH, AND OPENNESS TO RECONCILIATION.**

That's when she agreed to meet.

The three of us sat down for coffee a couple of weeks later. I listened to her talk about her personal life and the struggles that she was having. I empathised with her in those challenges. I confronted her about her ghosting behaviour and asked for an apology, which she gave me. I then reminded her of the amount she owed, which she then handed to me, all in cash.

As it turns out, she wasn't impoverished at all. Her personal issues were not financial. The money had been sitting in her bank account the whole time! The threat of a court case was what got her to the table.

I was annoyed, but I maintained my openness to reconcile. I thanked her and asked if there was anything I could do to support her. I offered to bring her in on a project I was looking at and told her that I would recommend her for it if it materialised.

She thanked me, we hugged (cuz I'm a hugger), and then we parted ways once again.

Attack and withdrawal are equally violent forms of communication, and both are intentional acts of unlove. These kinds of interactions are purpose-built to actively or passively disconnect one person from another.

CONFRONTING ATTACK AND WITHDRAWAL IN THE WORKPLACE

The most dramatic forms of attack are physical, sexual, psychological, and verbal abuse. As a leader, you should definitely put a stop to any of that in your workplace. But there are other more subtle ways in which those who prefer an attack strategy can express their violence.

Racist, sexist, or derogatory remarks count as an attack as well. Unfavourable comments about a person's physical or mental condition, or state of character, also fall into this category. These aren't acceptable behaviours for any respectable colleague. And it should be said that those in leadership set the tone for communication in an organisation and should be held to a higher standard than the majority of employees – not let off more easily due to their rank.

The most dramatic forms of withdrawal are social isolation, ghosting, and non-responsiveness – but because the only

> THOSE IN LEADERSHIP SET THE TONE FOR COMMUNICATION IN AN ORGANISATION AND SHOULD BE HELD TO A HIGHER STANDARD THAN THE MAJORITY OF EMPLOYEES – NOT LET OFF MORE EASILY DUE TO THEIR RANK.

evidence for withdrawal is a lack of communication, it can often be difficult to track in an organisation. It's when the team goes out for drinks to celebrate a birthday, but they don't invite the new guy "cuz he's a foreigner and might not 'fit in' with the rest of the team outside the office."

It's when Jenny's suggestions to her manager go unanswered, so after a couple of emails she gets the hint that she was hired because of the gender diversity policy and the boss isn't happy about it. His lack of reply is his way of expressing that she shouldn't be there. It's unloving.

On the most subtle side of attack and withdrawal are what some call microaggressions. This term was already in use more than four decades ago to describe "subtle, stunning, often automatic, and non-verbal exchanges which are 'put downs'" that African Americans experienced from White Americans.[121] In the years since, people have adopted other terms, such as subtle discrimination, subtle slight, or subtle acts of exclusion.[122]

---

121 Pierce, C. M., Carew, J. V., Pierce-Gonzalez, D., & Wills, D. (1977). An experiment in racism: TV commercials. *Education and Urban Society, 10*(1), 61-87, (p. 66).

122 Smith, I. A., & Griffiths, A. (2022). Microaggressions, everyday discrimination, workplace incivilities, and other subtle slights at work: A

I like the term "exclusionary behaviour,"[123] because to me it focusses on the core intent and/or effect of the behaviour: to exclude.

- An act/omission intended to exclude but not received as exclusionary is still exclusionary behaviour.
- An act/omission not intended to exclude but experienced as exclusionary is still exclusionary behaviour.

Exclusionary behaviours can be active or passive.

- Active exclusionary behaviours are an expression of attack.
- Passive exclusionary behaviours are an expression of withdrawal.

Exclusionary behaviours, however subtle, are at least as harmful as overt discrimination (**FP11.4**).[124] And one of the hardest

_____

    meta-synthesis. *Human Resource Development Review, 21*(3), 275-299.; Tiffany Jana, D. M., & Baran, M. (2020). *Subtle acts of exclusion: How to understand, identify, and stop microaggressions.* National Geographic Books.

123 Forrest, S., Eatough, V., & Shevlin, M. (2005). Measuring adult indirect aggression: The development and psychometric assessment of the indirect aggression scales. *Aggressive Behaviour: Official Journal of the International Society for Research on Aggression, 31*(1), 84-97.

124 Jones, K. P., Peddie, C. I., Gilrane, V. L., King, E. B., & Gray, A. L. (2016). Not so subtle: A meta-analytic investigation of the correlates of subtle and overt discrimination. *Journal of Management, 42*(6), 1588-1613.

things for leaders to do is to mediate when these social slights occur. Let's look at an example.

Nancy burst into James' office complaining that "Gerry's being sexist again! He's only using male pronouns when talking hypothetically about managers in the department."

Gerry stepped in only seconds behind her, already responding, "I'm sorry, Nancy. Honestly, the only reason I did that is because all of the managers in that department *are* males. It might not be fair, but it *is* true."

What is James to do? Is what Gerry said sexist?

To the females listening to all management speak in male terms, yes, probably it is. To the manager who's trying to describe the way things are, noting that those roles are currently occupied by men, no, probably not.

Was it exclusionary? Yes.

Was it intentional? No.

But this is the world we leaders live in now, and we need to know how to deal with it.

Researchers have proposed a four-dimensional framework for exclusionary behaviours that I find helpful. They suggest that leaders can approach these social slights by assessing four things:

1. Violation type: is it racist, sexist, anti-LGBTQ+, cultural, derogatory, etc?
2. Intensity: is it subtle condescending remarks or overt physical or verbal abuse (1-10 scale)?
3. Duration: is it a one-off event or sustained behaviour for months (1-10 scale)?
4. Intent: is it without motive, a cultural/language misunderstanding, or done with deliberate intent to harm? (**FP11.5**)[125]

I think these are helpful categories for leaders to look at when trying to determine the severity of an exclusionary behaviour. It also gives a starting place for the communicator and the receiver to have an open dialogue about what the piece of communication meant to each of them.

LOVE SEEKS RECONCILIATION

As I'm sure you've experienced, the same piece of communication can mean very different things to different people. Although the receiver has the right to determine for themselves the meaning of any piece of communication they receive, I've found it helpful to invite both the receiver and the communicator to

125 Smith, I. A., & Griffiths, A. (2022). Microaggressions, everyday discrimination, workplace incivilities, and other subtle slights at work: A meta-synthesis. Human Resource Development Review, 21(3), 275-299.

repeat back what happened in their own view, and then in the view of the other. This usually helps to highlight how misunderstandings might have occurred.

If it's not a misunderstanding but deliberately exclusionary behaviour, then for the sake of the economic community, that behaviour needs to be addressed, formally if required. Whether you call yourselves a company, community, tribe, or family, you should work towards love.

Love seeks to understand, confronts violence with truth, and actively pursues reconciliation (**FP11.6**).

ACTS OF UNLOVE IN THE WORKPLACE ARE OPPORTUNITIES FOR LEADERS TO FILL IN THE UNNECESSARY GAPS CAUSED BY EXCLUSIONARY BEHAVIOUR.

Acts of unlove in the workplace are opportunities for leaders to fill in the unnecessary gaps caused by exclusionary behaviour. As leaders we are often tempted to sweep them under the rug or ignore them as distractions, but addressing them head-on provides an opportunity for us to bring two or more diverse people together in a way that, if successful, will improve the quality of all our lives.

Remember, diversity is a best practise for quality decision making. When people who don't see eye to eye begin to value and respect each other, the quality of their work will go up. Ultimately, it's an investment in them as individuals, one that has a residual effect on the organisation through strengthening relationships.

I'm not suggesting that conflicting employees will suddenly love one another if they try to reconcile, but in my experience, all sincere pursuits of forgiveness and reconciliation are indistinguishable from love.

FIRST PRINCIPLES

FP11.1 Cancel culture is an example of unlove in the form of attack.

FP11.2 There are two kinds of unlove: attack and withdrawal.

FP11.3 Ghosting is an example of unlove in the form of withdrawal.

FP11.4 Attack and withdrawal can range from minor exclusionary behaviours all the way to violence.

FP11.5 The severity of an exclusionary behaviour can be judged by its type, intensity, duration, and intent.

FP11.6 Love confronts both attack and withdrawal with the truth and an openness to reconcile.

NEXT STEPS

1. Hold your leaders to a higher standard than others for inclusive communication in the workplace.

2. Can you remember a time when an exclusionary behaviour was highlighted for you and you ignored it or brushed it under the rug? What do you think was the result of that?
3. Remember a time when you participated in ghosting or cancel culture, how will you change your behaviour in the future?

LOVE LANGUAGE #2: WORDS OF AFFIRMATION

CHAPTER 12

LOVING LEADERSHIP

The Final Frontier of Empathy in Leadership

"THE ONLY SOURCE OF A LEADER'S POWER IS THAT OTHER PEOPLE CHOOSE TO FOLLOW THEM ... AND WHY WOULD THEY CHOOSE TO FOLLOW YOU? ... YOU WILL ONLY CHOOSE TO FOLLOW SOMEONE THAT: A) YOU BELIEVE WILL TAKE YOU TO A BETTER PLACE, AND B) THAT KNOWS YOU, CARES ABOUT YOU, TRUSTS YOU, WANTS TO CHALLENGE YOU, AND WANTS TO SEE YOU AT YOUR BEST. IF YOU SEE THAT SOMEONE HAS THE ABILITY TO TAKE YOU TO A BETTER PLACE, HAS A VISION FOR WHERE YOU CAN GO, AND TRUSTS YOU, AND CARES ABOUT YOU, AND LOVES YOU.

PEOPLE DON'T LIKE TO USE THE WORD LOVE, BUT LOVE IS AS IMPORTANT IN BUSINESS AS IT IS AT HOME, MAYBE MORE BECAUSE IT'S NOT EXPECTED IN BUSINESS. YOU'VE GOT TO LOVE YOUR PEOPLE, BECAUSE WHEN YOU LOVE YOUR PEOPLE THEY SAY, 'HEY WAIT, THIS GUY LOVES ME, THIS GUY CAN TAKE ME TO A BETTER PLACE,

AND IS GOING TO TAKE ME TO A BETTER PLACE.
I'M GONNA FOLLOW THIS LEADER.'"[126]

—MONTY MORAN, *CEO, CHIPOTLE MEXICAN GRILL*

LOVED = VALUED + RECIPROCITY
TIME (FP12.1)

TO BE LOVED OR TO BE FEARED

Leaders have been asking me recently if it's better to be loved or feared by their staff. It's a valid question. The answer in brief is that loving leadership is ultimately more effective, but let's look at why for a minute.

Leaders who lead with tough words, professional distance, and a fear-based strategy may achieve faster short-term compliance. That's because people whose livelihoods are being threatened might work hard to keep food on the plate and gas in the car, which could give the impression of loyalty to the leader and justification of their methods. So yes, tough leaders can get things done in the moment.

---

126 Moran, M., & Lakhiani, V. (n.d.). The power of love at work: How Monty Moran turned Chipotle into America's fav restaurant. *YouTube*. Retrieved from https://www.youtube.com/watch?v=_Ho8b7TFeH4.

But consider what fear-based leaders are missing out on. What is the long-term cost to a company in not having the following things?

1. Trust: When a leader is trusted by an employee, the latter is more likely to do what is required without challenging it, if they agree that the leader's instructions are helpful for the company. Fear-based leaders miss out on this efficiency.

2. Open Communication: When employees feel loved by their leader, they also feel comfortable sharing their feedback, new ideas, and concerns. Open communication empowers the leader with quicker access to relevant information, allowing for more informed decision making. Fear-based leaders pay the price of poor decision making associated with limited visibility of relevant information, and one bad decision at the highest level can cost millions of dollars.

3. Empowerment and Autonomy: A loving leader empowers their team members with the autonomy to make decisions within their areas of responsibility. The delegation of authority speeds up both decision making and execution processes by eliminating unnecessary hierarchical bottlenecks. Fear-based leaders don't trust their staff, and they accrue significant inefficiencies and missed opportunity costs associated with their need for control.

4. Collaboration and Teamwork: Loving leaders foster a culture of collaboration by encouraging team members to work together, leveraging the benefits of diversity of input, perspectives, and skills. Collaboration results in more innovative solutions and faster execution of plans. Fear-based

leaders are threatened by collaboration, because it often results in a loss of direct control over methodology or outcomes. Managing silos is easier work than leading empowered collaborators, but it leads the fear-based leader to cause bottlenecks.

5. Employee Motivation and Engagement: When employees feel loved and valued, they tend to be more intrinsically motivated, resulting in higher engagement in their work. Increased engagement translates into higher productivity and profitability, often due to the simple willingness of the employee to go the extra mile. Fear-based leaders aren't respected when they're not looking, so they pay the price by missing out on discretionary effort and real loyalty.

6. Adaptability and Flexibility: Loving leaders are often more adaptable and flexible in their decision making. They consider the wellbeing and needs of their people, allowing for changes to plans when necessary. This leadership agility enables quicker and more effective responses to challenges and opportunities. Fear-based leaders never hear from their teams the options available to them for rapid shifts in strategy, so they pay the price of never knowing something could have been done better.

It doesn't take a degree in organisational dynamics or finance to figure out that the costs associated with fear-based leadership are immense. Let me put a nail in this coffin right now: employees acting out of fear will do what they need to for survival; employees acting out of love will do everything in their power to achieve their leader's vision (**FP12.2**). Any leader who still thinks fear-based leadership is more effective than loving leadership is prioritising their own need for control over the profit of their company.

THE STATE OF LOVE IN LEADERSHIP

I've heard it said that effective leaders can lead out of *either* love *or* fear, and that some have tried to walk the imaginary line between them and evoke both kinds of motivation. Well, I hope by now you can tell which side of this debate I've landed on. There's no line between love and fear, there's only a chasm defined by different measures of distance in the areas of trust, transparency, intimacy, reciprocity, positivity resonance, and unconditional positive regard.

And this is not a breakthrough idea, either.

Already in 1992, John MacKey, co-founder of Whole Foods Market, famously claimed, "We are creating an organisation based on love instead of fear." He worked this idea into the leadership culture by starting meetings by having participants each appreciate one another for something, and by signing off his company-wide emails with "Love, John."[127]

---

127 Dutta, S. K. (2013). Whole Foods Market: A revolutionary management model at work. *Pacific Business Review International* 6(1), 15-24.

More recently Herb Kelleher, former CEO of SouthWest Airlines also caught the love-bug, stating that "a company is stronger if bound by love than by fear." Herb was hailed by Fortune Magazine as "perhaps the best CEO in America," and by Forbes as the creator of "the greatest success story in the history of commercial aviation."[128]

And Jack Ma said at the World Economic Forum's annual meeting in 2018, "To gain success a person will need high EQ; if you don't want to lose quickly you will need a high IQ, and if you want to be respected you need high LQ – the IQ of love."[129]

> **LOVING LEADERS INTENTIONALLY FOSTER AND DEVELOP THE EMOTIONAL CULTURE OF THEIR ORGANISATIONS.**

A few brave writers have dared the mirky waters of love at work before me. They've noted that loving leaders aren't just those who gain the "love" of followers through drama and charisma.[130] Loving leaders make a genuine effort to understand others, accept their own

---

128 Freiberg, K., & Freiberg, J. (2019). 20 reasons why Herb Kelleher was one of the most beloved leaders of our time. *Forbes*. Retrieved from https://www.forbes.com/sites/kevinandjackiefreiberg/2019/01/04/20-reasons-why-herb-kelleher-was-one-of-the-most-beloved-leaders-of-our-time/?sh=2d33bbddb311.

129 IQ means Intelligence Quotient; EQ means Emotional Intelligence; LQ means Love Intelligence. Jack Ma on the IQ of love – and other top quotes from his Davos interview. (2018). *World Economic Forum*. Retrieved from https://www.weforum.org/agenda/2018/01/jack-ma-davos-top-quotes/.

130 Parry, K. & Kempster, S. (2014). Love and leadership: Constructing follower narrative identities of charismatic leadership. *Management Learning, 45*(1), 21-38.

flaws, and create open space for tough conversations.[131] They intentionally foster and develop the emotional culture of their organisations.[132]

One such example is undoubtedly the late Frances Hesselbein, former CEO of the Girl Scouts of the USA. Management guru Stephen R. Covey called her "a pioneer for women, for diversity, and for leadership that changes lives. Frances is a model for living one's values." And Peter F. Drucker called her "the best CEO in America … She could manage any company in America, even General Motors, and do a great job."[133]

Her inclusive, understanding, empathetic and emotionally engaged leadership style provides an exemplary model for us to follow. The University of Pittsburgh's Graduate School of Public and International Affairs (GSPIA) launched the Frances Hesselbein Leadership Forum in 2017, and Dean Carissa Slotterback said that she "helped develop, amplify and demonstrate a conception of leadership that goes well beyond formal leadership positions and roles. She has truly helped all of us to understand that leadership is deeply personal and an act of love and care for others."[134]

131 Bonnevalle, N. (n.d.). Leading with love: Three ways leadership can show love in the workplace. https://www.thnk.org/blog/leading-with-love/.

132 Sigal, B., & O'Neill, O. (2014). Employees who feel love perform better. Retrieved from https://hbr.org/2014/01/employees-who-feel-love-perform-better?

133 Dr. Frances Hesselbein: Leading with a purpose. (2023). *DiversityWomanMedia*. Retrieved from https://www.diversitywoman.com/dr-frances-hesselbein-leading-with-a-purpose/.

134 Frances Hesselbein, a Pitt visionary and one of the world's "greatest leaders," has died at 107. (2022). *PittWire*. University of Pittsburg.

With each of these powerful voices pointing to Frances as a paragon, perhaps we should mind how she herself defined leadership: "It's a matter of how to be, not how to do. We spend most of our lives learning how to do and teaching other people how to do, yet it is the quality and character of the leader that determines the performance, the results."[135] Frances' leadership – what I and others call loving leadership – is a matter of character, of being.

Giants in the leadership space like Robert Greenleaf and Max De Pree have described leadership as an act of service by leaders towards their employees.[136] Stephen R. Covey has related love to trust as a quality of leadership.[137] United States Colonel Joe Riccardi has found that intimacy in relationships is the core of loving leadership.[138] Even authors Kouzes and Posner (2017) say in *The Leadership Challenge* that the secret ingredient in leadership is ultimately love.[139]

Retrieved from https://www.pitt.edu/pittwire/features-articles/frances-hesselbein-obituary.

135 Edersheim, E. (2017). The woman Drucker said was the best CEO in America. Retrieved from https://www.managementmattersnetwork.com/notable-quotable/columns/the-woman-drucker-said-was-the-best-ceo-in-america#:~:text=D.&text=Photo%3A%20Wesley%20Mann-,Peter%20F.,That%20was%20in%201990.

136 DePree, M. (2004). *Leadership is an art.* Crown; Greenleaf, R. K. (2015). *The Servant as Leader.* Greenleaf Center for Servant Leadership.

137 Covey, S. R. (1992). *Principle-centered leadership.* Simon & Schuster.

138 Ricciardi, J. A. (2014). *To lead is to love: An exploration into the role of love in leadership.* Benedictine University.

139 Kouzes, J. M., & Posner, B. Z. (2017). *The leadership challenge: How to get extraordinary things done in organisations* (6th ed.). Jossey-Bass.

Love has been explored and defined by a few leadership researchers, but it certainly hasn't received the attention that a concept this essential to the human experience deserves (**FP12.3**). Among the definitions of love in leadership I've surveyed, here are the ones I like most.

Love is "the sacred quality which enables individuals to willingly give of themselves to help others to achieve their highest potential and to create a better world,"[140] and "to love is to act intentionally, in sympathetic response to others … to promote individual and overall well-being."[141] These definitions are the closest to mine, though I think that the willingness to sacrifice of oneself is intrinsic to love as a quality in relationships. If you'll recall, my definition of love was pretty simple:

> Love is the willingness to reduce one's own quality of life in order to improve the quality of someone else's life.

This simple paradigm can help us define love as a leadership quality in an organisation. So when I adapt my definition of love to organisational leadership, this is what I come up with:

Loving Leadership is the willingness of a leader to use their available resources, including time, effort,

---

140 Anderson, V., Caldwell, C., & Barfuss, B. (2019). Love: The heart of leadership. *Graziadio Business Review*(2).

141 Blakeley, K., & Blakeley, C. (2021). *Leading with love: Rehumanising the workplace*. Routledge, (p. 22).

knowledge, and emotional intimacy, to improve the quality of life for those in their care. (FP12.4)

Loving Leadership is characterised by the pursuit of the following relationship characteristics in the workplace (**FP12.5**):

- Emotional Connection,
- Shared Values,
- Positive Interactions,
- Proper Physical Contact,
- Commitment,
- Transparency,
- Trust,
- Shared Experiences.

A loving leader can be identified by the levels of each of these qualities in their relationships with their employees and colleagues.

THE ROLE OF LOVE IN ACTIVE LISTENING

Peter F. Drucker once said, "most organisations need somebody who can lead regardless of the weather. What matters is that he or she works on the basic competencies. As the first such basic competence, I would put the willingness, ability, and self-discipline to listen. Listening is not a skill; it is a discipline. Anybody can do it. All you have to do is to keep your mouth shut. The second essential competence is the willingness to communicate, to make yourself understood. That requires infinite patience."[142]

Love in active listening goes beyond valuing the other person. Valuing someone involves listening for understanding; adding love to the formula requires the person to listen with the intent to act on behalf of the person speaking, to improve the quality of the other person's life. In this stage we move beyond listening for learning to listening for learning and altruism.

It's an act of gratitude when leaders, as listeners, understand and apply what they are receiving; it communicates valuation to those speaking. But we're talking about a whole new level when they use what they are learning to conspire on behalf of the person from whom they are learning it. In this way, loving leaders begin to bring their available resources to bear on improving the quality of the other person's life.

Okay, I think I can guess your next question:

Does that mean that if an employee asks for a ridiculous raise, I as a loving manager should just give it to them?

---

142 Drucker, P. F. (2009). *The daily Drucker: 366 days of insight and motivation for getting the right things done.* Harper Collins.

Short answer: No. Because that's not the loving thing to do. I'll explain …

Remember that loving leaders conspire to improve the quality of life for *those* in their care (*those*: plural). It's seldom possible to grant the wishes of the one without stealing from the many. As managers in our organisations, we need to take care of all of those in our care, not just the one in front of us today.

> **AS MANAGERS IN OUR ORGANISATIONS, WE NEED TO TAKE CARE OF ALL OF THOSE IN OUR CARE, NOT JUST THE ONE IN FRONT OF US TODAY.**

Clearly, it would improve the quality of one employee's life if we gave them a raise to half a million dollars a year in salary with six months of vacation every year. That would be great for them, but it would hurt the community a lot, and might even collapse the community altogether. This is where our all being part of a social species helps to form the boundaries of what can and should be lovingly done by a leader.

In a community, what's good for us should be good for all of us.

SHAREHOLDER SUPREMACY

CEOs of large companies must balance the felt needs of the employees with those of other stakeholder groups, including customers, vendors, and shareholders. But in the last half century, it's the shareholders who have been best cared for in our organisations. It's their voices that have been loudest and most listened to, and we need to correct that.

Just briefly: the shareholder supremacy movement began in 1970 when economist Milton Friedman proposed that companies existed for the sole purpose of generating shareholder value, which meant that the shareholders, not the employees, were the most important stakeholders in a company.[143] It was a popular view that led to many of our most horrible, dehumanising, and damaging management and organisational policies. We started calling our team members "human capital," viewing employees as disposable assets and variable expenses. Events like the Boeing 737 MAX crashes in 2018 and 2019 that killed 346 people were a natural result of Freidman's shareholder supremacy thesis (**FP12.6**).[144]

We can't give the shareholders whatever they want, and we can't give the employees whatever they want, either. Active listening in loving leadership doesn't mean that giving people

---

143 Friedman, M. (September 13, 1970). The social responsibility of business is to increase its profits. *New York Times Magazine*.

144 Block, C. (2022). Be a better leader among corporate personhood, shareholder supremacy and humans-as-resources. *Forbes*. I've critiqued Friedman elsewhere, so I won't repeat that here. See Block, C. J. (2019). The corporate social responsibility meme as a business foundation for economic peacemaking. In M. Lutfy & C. Toffolo (Eds.), *Handbook of Research on Promoting Peace Through Practice, Academia, and the Arts* (pp. 440-461). IGI Global.

whatever they want is the most loving thing to do, no matter who they are.

So whose needs do we need to balance?

STAKEHOLDER COMMUNITY

The needs that must be balanced by leaders in organisations are those defined in Robert Freeman's (1984) stakeholder theory as "any group or individual who can affect or is affected by the achievement of the organisation's objectives."[145] That's a pretty broad constituency; finding balance in that complex community might only be possible through loving leadership.[146]

This highlights one of the challenges leaders face in loving leadership. We need to be actively listening to each of those stakeholder groups, and there can be a lot of them.

We need to work to establish inclusive and accessible channels of open communication for each of our stakeholder groups and individuals to speak, feel heard and be understood.

---

145   Freeman, R. E. (1984). *Strategic management: a stakeholder approach.* Pitman, (p. 46).

146   Kaptein, M. (2022). The moral duty to love one's stakeholders. *Journal of Business Ethics, 180*(2), 813-827.

> WE NEED TO WORK TO ESTABLISH INCLUSIVE AND ACCESSIBLE CHANNELS OF OPEN COMMUNICATION FOR EACH OF OUR STAKEHOLDER GROUPS AND INDIVIDUALS TO SPEAK, FEEL HEARD AND BE UNDERSTOOD.

When we make meaningful changes to love and serve them better, in ways that serve the entire stakeholder community, they will each feel valued. Once they see that their voice is an indispensable quality of our relationship with them as stakeholders – and that it changes our behaviour as leaders and organisations – they will also be able to experience our active listening as an expression of loving leadership.

Fiduciary duties can conflict with your intention to be a loving leader, which can be challenging. Here are some strategies you might consider:

1. Clear Communication: Clearly communicate to the team the responsibilities and constraints associated with fiduciary duties. Help them understand the decision-making process and the reasons behind certain tough decisions. Transparency can maintain trust even in difficult times.
2. Ethical Decision Making: Ensure that decisions are ethical and align with the organisation's values. Even tough decisions can be made with integrity and respect for individuals involved.
3. Seek Win-Win Solutions: Explore creative solutions that balance fiduciary duties and a caring leadership approach.

This might involve finding ways to minimise negative impacts on the team while still meeting obligations.

4. Employee Support: Provide support to employees who are affected by these decisions. This could involve career counselling, job placement assistance, or other forms of support.

5. Empathy: Display empathy and concern for the team. Even when tough decisions must be made, showing that you understand and care about their impact can make a difference.

6. Learn and Grow: Use these experiences as opportunities to learn and improve both the business and your leadership approach.

It's all about balancing the legal and financial responsibilities with the human aspect of leadership. It's not always easy, but striving for such balance can lead to a healthier, more resilient organisation.

I know, I know. It's a lot to take in, but that's the nature of the connected world we've created for ourselves. So where do we start? We can start by loving the individual in front of us today, and we can do that with little to no expense if we speak their love language.

THE FIVE LOVE LANGUAGES

A helpful shorthand for expressing love as a leader to an individual can be found in relationship expert Gary Chapman's book *The Five Love Languages*.[147] I've been using his model for years because it's high-impact, low investment, and very easy to learn.

Chapman wrote for married couples, life partners, and others in long-term, committed (romantic) relationships. For the last few years I've been translating his work into my executive coaching practise and leadership training programs to help my clients express loving leadership.

Chapman found that people dominantly give and receive love in one of five common languages: gifts, words of affirmation, acts of service, quality time, and touch. Most people value all of them to some degree but one or two of them pre-dominantly (**FP12.7**).

You probably learned your dominant love language in childhood and use it with people unconsciously. I want you to use it intentionally at work, so try to pick out which is your most native love language.

Love Language #1: Gifts

Some people give and receive love by giving and receiving gifts.

---

147 Chapman, G. D. (2022). *The five love languages: How to express heartfelt commitment to your mate.* Lulu Press.

In the context of love at work, gifts might include an unsolicited raise or bonus, but also flowers or cake to celebrate a birthday, a trophy or prize to celebrate an achievement, or a cup of coffee bought as an act of appreciation and thoughtfulness.

These colleagues light up when their manager comes over to hand them a new company pen, shirt, or water bottle. They might decorate their workspaces with gifts they're received in the past, and they tend to not throw things away that were thoughtfully given by a co-worker, even if they don't particularly like them.

People who experience love in the language of gifts tend to like to arrange gifts for others as well. They're often the ones collecting money to purchase and present something nice to a colleague who has resigned or is going on maternity leave. And they tend to be the stewards of the office birthday calendar.

The challenge with expressing love at work with gifts is that sometimes gifts are against company policy, or the giving of a gift to one person creates expectations for everyone else. To avoid jealousy in the office (or adhere to a no-gifts policy), keep the gifts small and thoughtful. If you go for a coffee, bring them back one as well. If you receive something branded, or a sample from a vender that you don't need, pass it on to your gifts-loving team members. They'll appreciate it, and they'll experience it as an act of love from you.

And always make sure you remember their birthday! It's important to them. Gifts given at random times are valued as well, as it shows them that you were thinking of them when they were not around. And when it comes to the kinds of gifts they appreciate, it really is the thought that counts. The monetary value of a gift is not nearly as important as why that particular gift was chosen, or how it is presented to them.

Love Language #2: Words of Affirmation

Some people give and receive love by giving and receiving verbal praise.

In the context of love at work, affirmation is probably the easiest love language to communicate in. It's positive feedback, or unsolicited encouragement. It's when you tell someone what you like or appreciate about them as a person, or about what they've done.

> IN THE CONTEXT OF LOVE AT WORK, AFFIRMATION IS PROBABLY THE EASIEST LOVE LANGUAGE TO COMMUNICATE IN. IT'S POSITIVE FEEDBACK, OR UNSOLICITED ENCOURAGEMENT. IT'S WHEN YOU TELL SOMEONE WHAT YOU LIKE OR APPRECIATE ABOUT THEM AS A PERSON, OR ABOUT WHAT THEY'VE DONE.

It can include the brief words introducing an award for an employee, the glowing personal comment in their performance review, or a simple "great job on that project," from their manager. They love being told that what they do adds value to the organisation, to their team, and to their manager.

You'll recognise them because they are often thoughtful about how they express appreciation for others as well. They probably won't be able to pass through their work environment without complimenting someone else. They might write notes or send emails simply to express appreciation. And if they're a little love-deficient in their work environment, they might disguise their feeling of being unloved in a request for feedback, such as: "Hey, how am I doing this month?"

The challenge with affirmation-love employees is that they can sometimes be seen as suck-ups by other members of the team. They might tell the boss they like her new suit, or pop their head in to say something nice to their manager each day. Their praise is most likely genuine, though. They're expressing con- nectedness and love in a language that's native to them, but it still might be interpreted as "a little too much" by bosses or co-workers who don't value or speak affirmation naturally as a love language.

To express love to these employees, a regular point of contact and praise is usually enough. I encourage leaders to have a point of contact with each of their team members every day, a face-to-face once a week, and a team gathering once a month, as a benchmark. These are all opportunities for a quick "You're doing great!" or "Thanks for sending that email to our client, it was well written." These employees will read every word on a performance review or letter of reference and take them to heart as well, so be kind and generous with your words.

Love Language #3: Acts of Service

Some people give and receive love by doing things for others and appreciating things done for them.

You'll recognise such people at work because they'll be the helpful ones. They're the ones offering to support their team-mates in the little things. They will take on the last mile of a project, offer to go over a presentation with a colleague before it's submitted, or clean the breakroom when no one is looking.

They'll notice if someone brings them a cup of coffee, offers to take on a challenging client or project, finishes a report for them, or offers to hang their jacket for them. They'll hear any offer to help them as an offer of generosity, even if they don't accept the help. They will interpret a manager's moving the schedule around to give them a day off as love.

Managers typically view acts of service as something that should be provided by the employees to the manager. The employees are there to serve the boss, right? Well, I don't think so at all. I think the employees are there to serve the custom-ers and stakeholders of the company. And if the employees are serving the customers, who is serving the employees? That's right, their managers.

Robert Greenleaf got this right in *Servant Leadership* when he turned the organisation chart upside down.[148] The CEO serves the Executive Committee and the Chiefs serve the executives, who then serve the senior managers, who serve the junior managers, who then serve the front-line staff so they can serve the customers. Love is intrinsic to servant leadership; the greatest leader is the servant of all.[149]

The challenge with service-love teammates is that they too might be seen as currying favour. If they're genuinely feeling connected to their manager, they'll express it by doing little things to improve the quality of their manager's life and work. They might pick up extra work to do on the weekend, bring the boss a detox juice on a Monday morning, or offer to complete a part of their manager's report that the latter doesn't like to do. That can sometimes be misinterpreted as brown-nosing.

To express love towards these team members, look for little things you can do for them. Offer to help them finish up a spreadsheet, bring them a reference manual you know they'll need soon, or tell them you'll streamline a process or knock a task off their to-do list for them. They experience small favours as genuine love.

---

148 Greenleaf, R. K. (2002). *Servant leadership: A journey into the nature of legitimate power and greatness.* Paulist Press.

149 Buck, T. (2019). Love and servant-leadership. *The International Journal of Servant-Leadership, 13*(1), 287–312. Retrieved from https://www.proquest.com/scholarly-journals/love-servant-leadership/docview/2414424984/se-2.

Love Language #4: Quality Time

Some people give and receive love by spending quality time with people.

In the context of love at work, such people sacrifice the most valuable asset any worker has: their time. We all have only 24 hours each day, and once those hours are gone, we never get them back. Quality-time people offer their precious time as an expression of love.

You'll recognise them because they might come early and stay late – to work, to meetings, to coffee with a colleague. They will linger in the hallway after a meeting for the post-meeting meeting. Their preference is to work with others whenever possible, so they are natural collaborators. They often want frequent interactions (and/or long interactions) with their team members, direct reports, clients, vendors, and their line manager. They express love towards their team or organisation in time-on-task and discretionary effort.

The challenge with quality-time people is that they can appear needy. They might linger a little "too long" in the office, or at meetings. They might seem demanding, as they may request more meetings, as a subconscious expression of (or need for) love.

To express love towards them, remember that quality is better than quantity. Short meaningful touchpoints throughout the week will alleviate the need for longer meetings. Keep your communication with them as meaningful as possible, always asking about their personal life before talking about work. A simple one-on-one lunch with their manager will be received as a deep expression of love and value, and they're likely to work harder out of gratitude for time like that.

Love Language #5: Touch

Some people give and receive love through physical contact.

In the context of love at work, this may be the most difficult type to express consistently well, especially across cultures and genders. Touch-oriented people typically value shaking hands, or a pat on the back. They are quick to put their hand on the shoulder of a co-worker who appears upset, and might tap a colleague on the toe with their foot to gain their attention. Touch-oriented people express love with physical proximity.

You'll recognise them because they might be huggers like me. They'll be the first to offer a handshake, and they might double up on it with their other hand to express greater connection. They typically enjoy working in close proximity with others and will purposely choose the smallest table that can reasonably fit everyone.

The challenge with these co-workers is that what constitutes proper or acceptable touch is influenced a lot by gender and culture. What might be an appreciated expression of touch with a person of the same sex might not be appropriate with a person of the opposite sex. But if you make that assumption incorrectly, you risk having a touch-oriented teammate of the opposite sex feeling excluded and unloved (because they did not receive the same physical greetings as others).

To express love towards a touch-oriented person of the same gender, a handshake, a brief pat on the back, or a light tap on the back of the elbow is typically received as loving. In some cultures I've worked in hugs (USA) and kisses (Yemen, Egypt) are also acceptable among colleagues of the same sex. If you have any doubt, ask. A consent request allows the other person to decide how they want love expressed towards them. Don't assume too much with this love language, especially with clarity only a question away.

> **YOU PROBABLY KNOW BY NOW WHICH OF THE FIVE LANGUAGES IS YOUR NATIVE ONE. IT'S THE LANGUAGE YOU FEEL MOST VALUED IN WHEN OTHERS USE IT ON YOU, AND PROBABLY ALSO THE ONE THAT YOU USE THE MOST WHEN YOU WANT TO VALUE OTHERS.**

You probably know by now which of the five languages is your native one. It's the language that makes you feel most valued when others use it on you; it's probably the one you use the most when you want to value others. No one is naturally dominant in all of them and no one has none of them, but you might have two dominant love languages, depending on how you were raised as a child.

Some important things to know as a leader:

1. You'll naturally tend to connect more deeply with people whose love languages are the same as your own. They'll naturally communicate with you in a way that you appreciate, and you'll naturally do the same with them.
2. You'll find connecting more difficult with people who have different native love languages. Their communications of love might go completely unnoticed by you, and your communications of love might go undervalued by them, leaving both of you with subtle feelings of disconnectedness and possibly frustration.
3. You can learn to express love in a language that is not native or natural to you; as a leader you'll benefit greatly if you learn to do so.
4. Expressions of love are never malicious. They are simply either expressions of love or requests for love.

It is a powerful leadership skill to be able to understand and speak all five languages. Can you imagine the influence you will have with your team, your colleagues, and your line manager once you intentionally speak each of their love languages at work? Make a game for yourself of trying to figure everyone out. Run experiments on them to see what they respond to the most, and pay attention to how they communicate in their other close relationships at work.

IF YOU WANT TO FEEL LOVED, LOVE

Would it improve the quality of your life if you truly loved the people you work with? Would it improve the quality of your life if you knew that they truly loved you too? How can you get from where you are now with co-workers (hopefully already feeling valued by you), to a place where they feel loved by you as a leader?

It's simple: add reciprocity over time. Make the relationship reciprocal by continuously inviting their voice to influence you; exhibit the kind of change that improves the quality of their life, and then expect them to do the same. Over time, the deepening of mutual influence founded on genuine curiosity and care will form a sense of commitment between you that will dissolve the professional distance you've been taught to protect.

Professional distance at its best protects others from our values, but love occurs when we embrace others in spite of our differing values. We no longer need to protect each other from our values, because we prize them in each other – we see them as a part of our diverse individuality. We can be *together* instead of being *right*, and we can understand one another without needing to agree on everything.

Loving Leadership is the willingness of a leader to use their available resources, including time, effort, knowledge, and emotional intimacy, to improve the quality of life for those in their care. It is the natural course of mutually supportive relationships between human beings, and it is the most powerful quality of leadership.

FIRST PRINCIPLES

FP12.1 LOVED = VALUED + RECIPROCITY / TIME

FP12.2 It is more profitable in the long term to be loved than feared in leadership.

FP12.3 Love in leadership theory is not a new thing, but it hasn't received the attention it deserves.

FP12.4 Loving Leadership is the willingness of a leader to use their available resources, including time, effort, knowledge, and emotional intimacy, to improve the quality of life for those in their care.

FP12.5 Loving leaders intentionally develop the emotional culture of their organisations.

FP12.6 Shareholder supremacy is an unloving management philosophy because it is by nature exclusive of all other stakeholder groups in an organisation.

FP12.7 People pre-dominantly give and receive love in one of five love languages: gifts, affirmation, service, time, and touch.

NEXT STEPS

1. Map out all the stakeholder groups in your organisation, and make sure they all have channels for communicating and receiving feedback.
2. Identify any stakeholders you have not been very good at loving and choose behaviours that will help them to feel loved by you.
3. Identify your dominant love language.
4. Identify the dominant love languages of your team at work, including your colleagues and your boss. What can you do to lead them in a more loving way?

IMAGINE LOVE AT WORK

CONCLUSION

Imagine All the People

IMAGINE LOVE AT WORK

I was sitting with another coach in Dubai recently, discussing one of our mutual clients, a major family company in fashion and entertainment with about 3,000 employees. I praised the company's Head of Learning and Development, Hana, to which my colleague replied, "Hana, yes! I love her! She's really amazing."

So I asked, "Do you really?"

"Really what?"

"Really *love* Hana?" I smiled coyly.

"Well, you know. No. Well, yes. Yes, actually I suppose I do, otherwise I wouldn't have said it."

"Good. That's a good thing. Have you ever told her?"

"That I love her?! Oh, God no! Could you imagine?" he laughed.

But yes, yes, I could imagine.

- I imagine our corporate cultures behaving like the best possible versions of economic human communities.
- I imagine the most life-giving form of human belonging and connectedness as a common expression in the organisations in which humans spend the majority of their time.
- I imagine critical feedback sessions with struggling employees starting with their manager saying, "First of all, you are loved here, and I want to help you to perform at your natural best in our community."
- I imagine board meetings where the decisions are steered by the guiding question: "Is this the most loving thing that we can do to balance the felt needs of all of our stakeholders?"
- I imagine the word love beginning to appear on lists of corporate values on the About Us pages of company websites, in descriptions of employees in their letters of reference, and as filtering words when the applicant tracking system is shortlisting CVs for key leadership roles.
- I imagine executives walking out of the boardroom with a casual "I love you" to each of their colleagues. Not an insulated "I love you, man," or "I love what you did in there," or "I love your idea," but an honest and direct expression of love for one another.

I have to believe in the possibility of the honest and transparent reflection of mutual respect and valuation; in a commitment to conspire on behalf of one another when the other isn't looking; in the unamended acknowledgement of the foundation of trust that exists between two executives when, even after a challenging conversation, they make eye contact for a few seconds and affirm each other out loud with,

"I love you."

"I love you, too."

I imagine that. Can you?

READ THE MAP

I grew up in a time when love was emphasised in familial and social relationships but not in the professional realm. Yet in recent years I've been questioning why love is excluded from the workplace, especially for leaders who aim to improve the lives of their employees. Throughout this book we've explored together the importance of love in all aspects of life, including the workplace.

Remember that work is not just a job but a significant part of life. It should be meaningful, a way to express gratitude for the opportunities and resources you have been given. We've together acknowledged the challenges of love, drawing from personal experiences and professional stories.

We've trekked through this territory using the Love@Work roadmap, which is divided into three parts: Stepping from Darkness to Light, Marching towards Connectedness, and Running into Love at Work.

Part 1 addressed four key questions, concerning the impact of a lack of love in workplaces, the relationship between love and professional distance, the definition of love in the workplace, and the roadmap from the current state to the desired state of Love@Work.

Part 2 focused on the first four of the five stages of connectedness: inclusion, being heard, being understood, and being valued. Each stage was discussed in detail, along with the impact on individuals and organisations, which I hope was valuable for you. Along the way I attempted to provide practical tools and tips for leaders like yourself to facilitate each stage of connectedness.

Part 3 addressed two critical concerns that may arise when pursuing a more loving workplace: sex and romance at work, and attack and withdrawal as forms of unlove. We also discussed boundaries, workplace harassment, and the importance of reconciliation.

Finally, in Chapter 12, we explored the concept of loving leadership, including its impact on workplace culture. We looked at the qualities of a loving leader and specific ways to express love at work.

Thank you so much for embarking on this journey with me. I acknowledge that I don't have all the answers, but I am nevertheless committed to continuing to explore the importance of love in the workplace and the challenges it may entail. This conversation reflects the need to confront the darkness that exists without love. Love@Work can bring untold benefits to individuals who will live happier, healthier, and longer lives as a result of working in more loving workplaces. I'm convinced, as I hope you are now too, that these benefits will also result in better communication, connectivity, productivity, performance, and profitability.

COMMODIFICATION OF LOVE

Here's my final concern. Having written a book on love in the workplace and loving leadership, I'm afraid that "love" might just become the next big fad. That love, like happiness, empathy, and servanthood, will become commoditised. Consultancies will spring up with seven-stage plans for turning average organisational leaders into loving leaders. They'll box it up, wrap it in a nice package and put a price-tag on it, as though love can be taught, bought, or even sought.

Did you know you can already get your company certified as a Most Loved Workplace?[150]

---

150 Most Loved Workplace. (n.d.). What is the psychology of love in leadership? Retrieved from https://mostlovedworkplace.com/what-is-the-psychology-of-love-in-leadership/.

There's no clearly laid out strategy for becoming a more loving leader. There are no KPIs for Love@Work, though my friend Jeff Smith (The KPI Guy) will undoubtedly know exactly how to write them. And there's no ROI algorithm for Love@Work, though I'm confident that my friend Jack Phillips (Founder of The ROI Institute) will know exactly how to calculate it. I'm open to learning, but I'm pretty sure the commodification of love at work will lead just as often to rejection of the idea as acceptance.

My hope is that you, as a leader, will recognise that love isn't something that needs to be taught at all. This book didn't teach you anything you didn't already know in some other context, in relationships with your sibling, parent, or best friend.

It's all been inside you this whole time. And I'm willing to bet that even though the application of love at work might be a new concept for you, the principles and stages I outlined felt like fresh air to you when you read them. They made sense to you. Because love is your native language, and the suppression of it is foreign, not the other way around.

You, like each of the other leaders in your organisation, are the product of a million years of successful survival, adaptation, and collaboration. You have within you both the intrinsic need and ultimate capacity for love that have helped each of the last 10,000 generations of your ancestors to survive.

You don't need a manual for that. You just need to be told that it's okay to pursue love at work. It's the most natural thing. Many have tried to remove love from our organisations through social isolation, professional distance, and cold leadership principles. But that has robbed you of the possibility of having the richest human experience you've ever had in the place you spend the majority of your time with other humans: at work.

Well, let this book be your letter of permission to try another path.

WHAT IS THE LOVING THING TO DO?

Start by expressing love towards those you claim to lead. If you really are a loving leader, you'll actively curate an inclusive space where each of them feels safe to raise their voice and is acknowledged for doing so. Listening with curiosity and care will provide the echo each needs to hear from you to feel understood; and as you apply what you've learned from them, they'll also feel valued.

Finally, when you truly value your economic tribe as individuals and as a community, as their voices shape who you become and your voice shapes them in return, you might find yourself recognising that you love your team – perhaps less than you do your children, but far more than you do your favourite candy bar.

The most natural thing for you to say then might be,

"I love you, all of you. Now let's review our KPIs from the last quarter."

When in doubt about how to lead, let the instinct that guided your ancestors lead you in how to behave with those in your care. Ask yourself, "What's the loving thing to do?"

You'll know what to do. Why?

Because love has always been at work. We all know it. We've always known it.

All I've done is to say it out loud.

Now it's your turn to say it out loud.

I love you.

BIBLIOGRAPHY

35 employees kill themselves. Will their bosses go to jail? (2019). *The Business Times.* https://www.businesstimes.com.sg/startups-tech/technology/35-employees-kill-themselves-will-their-bosses-go-jail.

Adams, T., Reinert, M., Fritze, D., & Nguyen, T. (2021). Mind the workplace: Work health survey 2021.

Anderson, V., Caldwell, C., & Barfuss, B. (2019). Love: The heart of leadership. *Graziadio Business Review, 22*(2).

Ashford, S. J., & Cummings, L. L. (1983). Feedback as an individual resource: Personal strategies of creating information. *Organisational and Human Performance, 32*(3), 370-398.

Baumeister, R., & Leary, M. (1995). The need to belong: Desire for interpersonal attachments as a fundamental human motivation. *Psychological Bulletin, 117*(3), 497-529.

Barsade, S. G., & O'Neill, O. A. (2014). What's love got to do with it? A longitudinal study of the culture of companionate love and employee and client outcomes in a long-term care setting. *Administrative Science Quarterly, 59*(4), 551-598. https://doi.org/10.1177/0001839214538636.

Blakeley, K., & Blakeley, C. (2021). *Leading with love: Rehumanising the workplace.* Routledge.

Block, C. (2022). Be a better leader among corporate personhood, shareholder supremacy and humans-as-resources. *Forbes.*

Block, C. J. (2019). The corporate social responsibility meme as a business foundation for economic peacemaking. In M. Lutfy & C. Toffolo (Eds.),

Handbook of Research on Promoting Peace Through Practice, Academia, and the Arts (pp. 440-461). IGI Global. https://doi.org/10.4018/978-1-5225-3001-5.ch022.

Boekhorst, J.A. (2015). The role of authentic leadership in fostering workplace inclusion: A social information processing perspective. *Human Resource Management, 54*(2), 241. Retrieved from https://www.proquest.com/scholarly-journals/role-authentic-leadership-fostering-workplace/docview/1666454004/se-2.

Bollendorf, S. (2013). *Le grand incendie.* Retrieved from http://www.samuel-bollendorff.com/fr/le-grand-incendie-2/.

Buck, T. (2019). Love and servant-leadership. *The International Journal of Servant-Leadership, 13*(1), 287-312.

Buckingham, M. (2022). *Love + work: How to find what you love, love what you do, and do it for the rest of your life.* Harvard Business Review Press.

Burgard, S. A., Brand, J. E., & House, J. S. (2007). Toward a better estimation of the effect of job loss on health. *Journal of Health and Social Behaviour 2007, 48*(December), 369-384.

Burris, E. R., Detert, J. R., & Romney, A. C. (2013). Speaking up vs. being heard: The disagreement around and outcomes of employee voice. *Organisation Science, 24*(1), 22-38.

Buzzanell, P. M., & Dohrman, R. L. (2009). Supervisors, subordinates, and coworkers. In W. F. Eadie (Ed.), *21st century communication: A reference handbook.* Sage.

Bzdok, D., & Dunbar, R.I.M. (2022). Social isolation and the brain in the pandemic era. *Nature Human Behaviour, 6*, 1333-1343.

Cain, A. (2021). The business case for diversity and inclusion in the workplace. *Australian Restructuring Insolvency & Turnaround Association Journal, 33*(2), 34-37.

Carr, Austin. (2020). The cruise ship suicides. *Bloomberg.* Retrieved from https://www.bloomberg.com/features/2020-cruise-ship-suicides/.

Chapman, G. D. (2022). *The five love languages: How to express heartfelt commitment to your mate.* Northfield Publishing.

Cherniss, C., & Goleman, D. (2001). *The emotionally intelligent workplace: How to select for measure, and improve emotional intelligence in individuals, groups, and organisations.* Jossey-Bass.

Covey, S. R. (1992). *Principle-centered leadership.* Simon & Schuster.

CPP. (2008). Workplace conflict and how businesses can harness it to thrive.

Daw, Stephen. (2020). A complete timeline of Kevin Hart's Oscar-hosting controversy, from tweets to apologies. Billboard Media. https://www.billboard.com/music/awards/kevin-hart-oscar-hosting-controversy-timeline-8492982/.

De Aquino, C. T. E., & Robertson, R. W. (2018). *Diversity and inclusion in the global workplace.* Springer.

Delloitte, Female Quotient. (2018). Redefining Leadership. The Inclusion Imperative.

DePree, M. (2004). *Leadership is an art.* Crown.

DeRanieri, J. T., Clements, P. T., & Henry, G. C. (2002). When catastrophe happens: Assessment and intervention after sudden traumatic death. Journal of Psychosocial Nursing, 40(4), 30-37.; Mericle, B. P. (1993). When a colleague commits suicide. Journal of Psychosocial Nursing, 31(9), 11-13.

Detert, J. R., Trevino, L. K., & Sweitzer, V. L. (2008). Moral disengagement in ethical decision making: A study of antecedents and outcomes. *Journal of Applied Psychology, 93*(2), 374-391.

Diamandis, P. H., & Kotler, S. (2014). *Abundance.* Free Press.

Diem, W. (2009). Unions blame work pressure for suicides at Renault. Retrieved from https://www.wardsauto.com/news-analysis/unions-blame-work-pressure-suicides-renault.

Dixon-Fyle, S., Dolan, K., Hunt, V., & Prince, S. (2020). *Diversity wins: How inclusion matters.* McKinsey & Company.

Dr. Frances Hesselbein: Leading with a purpose. (2023). *DiversityWomanMedia.* Retrieved from https://www.diversitywoman. com/dr-frances-hesselbein-leading-with-a-purpose/.

Drucker, P. F. (2009). *The daily Drucker: 366 days of insight and motivation for getting the right things done.* Harper Collins.

Duncan, K. (2023). Survey: Compensation is the top factor of work-related stress in 2023. *JobSage.* Retrieved from https://www.jobsage. com/blog/survey-employees-mental-health-in-2023/.

Dutta, S. K. (2013). Whole Foods Market: A revolutionary management model at work. *Pacific Business Review International, 6*(1), 15-24.

Edersheim, E. (2017). The woman Drucker said was the best CEO in America. Retrieved from https://www.managementmattersnetwork. com/notable-quotable/columns/the-woman-drucker-said-was-the-best-ceo-in-america#:~:text=D.&text=Photo%3A%20Wesley%20 Mann-,Peter%20F.,That%20was%20in%201990.

Eisenberger, N. I. (2015). Social pain and the brain: Controversies, questions, and where to go from here. *Annual Review of Psychology, 66,* 601-629.

Eisenberger, N. I. (2012). The pain of social disconnection: Examining the shared neural underpinnings of physical and social pain. *Nature Reviews Neuroscience, 13*(6), 421-434.

Elsesser, K., & Peplau, L. A. (2006). The glass partition: Obstacles to cross-sex friendships at work. *Human Relations, 59*(8), 1077-1100. Retrieved from https://www.proquest.com/scholarly-journals/glass-partition-obstacles-cross-sex-friendships/docview/231455579/se-2.

Employees reveal absurd company regulations. (2011). *Japan Today.* Retrieved from https://japantoday.com/category/features/kuchikomi/ employees-reveal-absurd-company-regulations.

Forrest, S., Eatough, V., & Shevlin, M. (2005). Measuring adult indirect aggression: The development and psychometric assessment of the indirect aggression scales. *Aggressive Behaviour: Official Journal of the International Society for Research on Aggression, 31*(1), 84-97.

Frances Hesselbein, a Pitt visionary and one of the world's "greatest leaders," has died at 107. (2022). *PittWire*. University of Pittsburg. Retrieved from https://www.pitt.edu/pittwire/features-articles/frances-hesselbein-obituary.

Freeman, R. E. (1984). *Strategic management: a stakeholder approach*. Pitman.

Freiberg, K., & Freiberg, J. (2019). 20 reasons why Herb Kelleher was one of the most beloved leaders of our time. *Forbes*. Retrieved from https://www.forbes.com/sites/kevinandjackiefreiberg/2019/01/04/20-reasons-why-herb-kelleher-was-one-of-the-most-beloved-leaders-of-our-time/?sh=2d33bbddb311.

Friedman, M. (September 13, 1970). The social responsibility of business is to increase its profits. *New York Times Magazine*.

Gallo, W. T., Bradley, E. H., & Falba, T. A. (2004). Involuntary job loss as a risk factor for subsequent myocardial infarction and stroke: Findings from the Health and Retirement Survey. *American Journal of Industrial Medicine, 45*(5), 408–416.

Gallo, W. T., Teng, H.-M., Falba, T. A., Kasl, S. V., Bradley, E. H., & Krumholz, H. M. (2006). The impact of late career job loss on myocardial infarction and stroke: A 10-year follow up using the Health and Retirement Survey. *Journal of Occupational Environmental Medicine, 63*(10), 683-687.

Gallup. (2019). 8 behaviours of the world's best managers. Retrieved from https://www.gallup.com/workplace/272681/habits-world-best-managers.aspx.

Garcy, A. M., & Vågerö, D. (2013). Unemployment and suicide during and after a deep recession: A longitudinal study of 3.4 million Swedish men and women. *American Journal of Public Health, 103*(6), 1031-1038.

Garg, S., & Sangwan, S. (2021). Literature review on diversity and inclusion at workplace, 2010-2017. *Vision, 25*(1), 12-22.

Garnett, M. F., Curtin, S. C., & Stone, D. M. (2022). Suicide mortality in the United States, 2000-2020.

Glint. (2021). State of the manager. Retrieved from https://www.glintinc.com/wp-content/uploads/2021/03/State_of_the_Manager_2021.pdf.

Greenleaf, R. K. (2002). *Servant leadership: A journey into the nature of legitimate power and greatness* (25th anniversary edition). Paulist Press.

Greenleaf, R. K. (2015). *The Servant as Leader.* Greenleaf Center for Servant Leadership.

Grossman, D. (July 17, 2011). The cost of poor communications. *The Holmes Report.*

Hamilton, D. (2010). Top ten email blunders that cost companies money. *Creative Communications & Training.*

Harrison, R. (2008). Accessing the power of love in the workplace. Unpublished Manuscript. Freeland, WA. (p. 2). Retrieved from https://bschool.pepperdine.edu/masters-degree/organization-development/content/poweroflove.pdf.

Harter, C.J.J. (2019). *It's the Manager.* Gallup Press.

Hedegaard, H., & Warner, M. (2021). Suicide mortality in the United States, 1999-2019.

Henriksen, J., Larsen, E., Mattisson, C., & Andersson, N. (2019). Loneliness, health and mortality. *Epidemiology and Psychiatric Sciences, 28*(2), 234-239.

Hooton, C. (2018). Netflix film crews "banned from looking at each other for longer than five seconds" in #metoo crackdown. *Independent.* Retrieved from https://www.independent.co.uk/arts-entertainment/tv/news/netflix-sexual-harassment-training-rules-me-too-flirting-on-set-a8396431.html.

Howard, M. C., Follmer, K. B., Smith, M. B., Tucker, R. P., & Van Zandt, E. C. (2022). *Work and suicide: An interdisciplinary systematic literature review. Journal of Organisational Behaviour, 43*(2), 260-285 (p. 266).

Hunt, V., Layton, D., & Prince, S. (2015). Diversity matters. *McKinsey & Company, 1*(1), 15-29.

Hunt, V., Prince, S., Dixon-Fyle, S., & Yee, L. (2018). Delivering through diversity. *McKinsey & Company, 231*, 1-39.

International Labour Organisation. (1951). Equal remuneration convention (No. 100). Geneva, Switzerland.

International Labour Organisation. (1958). Discrimination (employment and occupation) convention (No. 111). Geneva, Switzerland.

International Labour Organisation. (1981). Workers with family responsibilities convention (No. 156). Geneva, Switzerland.

International Labour Organisation. (1983). Vocational rehabilitation and employment (disabled persons) convention (No. 159). Geneva, Switzerland.

International Labour Organisation. (1989). Indigenous and tribal peoples convention (No. 169). Geneva, Switzerland.

International Labour Organisation. (2000). Maternity protection convention (No. 183). Geneva, Switzerland.

International Labour Organisation. (2010). HIV and AIDS recommendation (No. 2000). Geneva, Switzerland.

International Labour Organisation. (2019). Elimination of violence and harassment in the world of work convention (No. 190). Geneva, Switzerland.

Jack Ma on the IQ of love – and other top quotes from his Davos interview. (2018). World Economic Forum. Retrieved from https://www.weforum.org/agenda/2018/01/jack-ma-davos-top-quotes/.

Jana, T., & Baran, M. (2020). *Subtle acts of exclusion: How to understand, identify, and stop microaggressions.* National Geographic Books.

Janske H. W. Eersel, Toon W. Taris & Paul A. Boelen (2020) Reciprocal relations between symptoms of complicated grief, depression, and anxiety following job loss: A cross-lagged analysis. *Clinical Psychologist, 24*(3), 276-284.

Janssens, M., Sels, L., & Van den Brande, I. (2003). Multiple dimensions of communication and their influence on employee commitment. *Journal of Business and Psychology, 17*(3), 377-390.

Jones, K. P., Peddie, C. I., Gilrane, V. L., King, E. B., & Gray, A. L. (2016). Not so subtle: A meta-analytic investigation of the correlates of subtle and overt discrimination. *Journal of Management, 42*(6), 1588-1613.

Kaptein, M. (2022). The moral duty to love one's stakeholders. *Journal of Business Ethics, 180*(2), 813-827.

Karren, R. (2012). Introduction to the special issue on job loss. *Journal of Managerial Psychology, 27*(8), 772-779.

Kasl, S., & Jones, B. (2000). The impact of job loss and retirement on health. In L. F. Berkman & I. Kawachi (Eds.), *Social epidemiology.* Oxford University Press.

Kerrissey, M. J., Hayirli, T. C., Bhanja, A., Stark, N., Hardy, J., & Peabody, C. R. (2022). How psychological safety and feeling heard relate to burnout and adaptation amid uncertainty. *Health Care Management Review, 47*(4), 308-316.

Kirby, E. L., Wieland, S., & McBride, M. C. (2013). Work-life communication. In J. G. Oetzel & S. Ting-Toomey (Eds.), *The Sage handbook of conflict communication: Integrating theory, research, and practice* (2nd ed., pp. 377-402). Sage.

Koerner, A. F., & Floyd, K. (2010). Evolutionary perspectives on interpersonal relationships. *New directions in interpersonal communication research,* 27-47.

Kouzes, J. M., & Posner, B. Z. (2017). *The leadership challenge: How to make extraordinary things happen in organisations.* Jossey-Bass.

Krams, I. (2016). Reciprocal altruism (middle-Level theory in evolutionary psychology). In: Weekes-Shackelford, V., Shackelford, T., (eds) *Encyclopedia of Evolutionary Psychological Science.* Springer.

Kurland N.B. & Bailey D.E. (1999). When workers are here, there, and everywhere: A discussion of the advantages and challenges of telework. *Organisational Dynamics, 28*(2), 53-68.

Kurland, N. B., & Cooper, C. D. (2002); Manager control and employee isolation in telecommuting environments. *The Journal of High Technology Management Research, 13*(1), 107-126.

Manavis, S. (July 16, 2020) "Cancel culture" does not exist. Available at: https://www.newstatesman.com/science-tech/2020/07/cancel-culture-does-not-exist (accessed 31 March 2023).

Mann, A. (2018). Why we need best friends at work. Retrieved from https://www.gallup.com/workplace/236213/why-need-best-friends-work.aspx.

Martin, M. W. (1997). Professional distance. *International Journal of Applied Philosophy, 11*(2) 39-50.

Marshall, G. W., Michaels, C. E., & Mulki, J. P. (2007). Workplace isolation: Exploring the construct and its measurement. *Psychology & Marketing, 24*(3), 195-223 (p. 198).

Maxwell, J. C. (1960). *The 5 levels of leadership.* Center Street.

McBride, M.C. & Bergen K.M. (2015) Work spouses: Defining and understanding a "new" relationship. *Communication Studies, 66*(5), 487-508.

McBride, M.C., Thorson, A.R. & Bergen K.M. (2020). An examination of individually performed and (co) managed facework: Unique communication within the work-spouse relationship. *Communication Studies, 71*(4), 489-510.

Merchant, Brian. (2017). The one device: the secret history of the iPhone. *Little, Brown and Company.*

Morrison, E. W., & Milliken, F. J. (2000). Organisational silence: A barrier to change and development in a pluralistic world. *Academy of Management Review, 25*(4), 706-725.

Noelke, C., & Beckfield, J. (2014). Recessions, job loss, and mortality among older US adults. *American Journal of Public Health, 104*(11), 126-134.

Monsour, M., Harris, B., Kurzwell, N., & Beard, C. (1994). Challenges confronting cross-sex friendships: "Much ado about nothing?" *Sex Roles, 37*, 825-845.

Moran, M., & Lakhiani, V. (n.d.). The power of love at work: How Monty Moran turned Chipotle into America's fav restaurant. *YouTube.* Retrieved from https://www.youtube.com/watch?v=_Ho8b7TFeH4.

Most Loved Workplace. (n.d.). What is the psychology of love in leadership? Retrieved from https://mostlovedworkplace.com/what-is-the-psychology-of-love-in-leadership/.

Ng, E. (2020). No grand pronouncements here: Reflections on cancel culture and digital media participation. *Television & New Media, 21*(6): 621-627.

Nicolas, L. (2020). Will HR need a hugging policy when employees return to the office? *Unleash.* Retrieved from https://www.unleash.ai/covid-19/when-can-we-hug-again/.

Nielsen, T. C., & Kepinski, L. (2016). Inclusion nudges guidebook: Practical techniques for changing behaviour, culture & systems to mitigate unconscious bias and create inclusive organisations. *CreateSpace.*

Novacek, G., et al. (2023). Inclusion isn't just nice, it's necessary. How a survey quantifying the responses of more than 27,000 employees proves the business value of inclusion. *Boston Consulting Group.*

O'Neill, O., & Rothbard, N.P. (2017). Is love all you need? The effects of emotional culture, suppression, and work-family conflict on firefighter risk-taking and health. *Academy of Management Journal, 60*(1), 78-108.

O'Neill, O. (2018). The FACCTs of (work) life: How relationships (and returns) are linked to the emotional culture of companionate love. *American Journal of Health Promotion, 32*(5), 1312-1315.

O'Súilleabháin P.S., Gallagher S., Steptoe A. (2019). Loneliness, living alone, and all-cause mortality: The role of emotional and social loneliness in the elderly during 19 years of follow-up. *Psychosomatic Medicine, 81*(6), 521-526.

Parry, K. & Kempster, S. (2014). Love and leadership: Constructing follower narrative identities of charismatic leadership. *Management Learning, 45*(1), 21-38.

Parsonage, M., & Saini, G. (2017). Mental health at work. Center for Mental Health.

Pfeffer, J., & Carney, D. R. (2018). The economic evaluation of time can cause stress. *Academy of Management Discoveries, 4*(1), 74-93.

Pierce, C. M., Carew, J. V., Pierce-Gonzalez, D., & Wills, D. (1977). An experiment in racism: TV commercials. *Education and Urban Society, 10*(1), 61-87.

Pinker, S. (2007). *The stuff of thought: Language as a window into human nature.* Viking.

Pinker, S. (2012). *The better angels of our nature.* Penguin.

Rafferty, A. E., Jimmieson, N. L., & Armenakis, A. A. (2013). Change readiness: A multilevel review. *Journal of Management, 39*(1), 110-135.

Ranseth, J. (2015). Gandhi didn't actually ever say "Be the change you want to see in the world." Here's the real quote. Retrieved from https://josephranseth.com/gandhi-didnt-say-be-the-change-you-want-to-see-in-the-world/.

Reis, H. T., & Shaver, P. (1988). Intimacy as an interpersonal process. *Handbook of Personal Relationships*, 367-389.

Robinson, B. (2019) New study says workplace bullying on the rise: What you can do during National Bullying Prevention Month. *Forbes*. Retrieved from https://www.forbes.com/sites/bryanrobinson/2019/10/11/new-study-says-workplace-bullying-on-rise-what-can-you-do-during-national-bullying-prevention-month/?sh=821fdb32a0d4.

Romansky, L., Garrod, M., Brown, K., & Deo, K. (2021). How to measure inclusion in the workplace. *Harvard Business Review*, 27.

Ricciardi, J. A. (2014). *To lead is to love: An exploration into the role of love in leadership.* Benedictine University.

Romano, A. (December 30, 2020). Why we can't stop fighting about cancel culture. Available at: https://www.vox.com/culture/2019/12/30/20879720/what-is-cancel-culture-explainedhistory-debate (accessed 31 March 2023).

Sahai, S., Ciby, M. A. & Kahwaji, A. (2020). Workplace Isolation: A systematic review and synthesis. *International Journal of Management, 11.*

Sapolsky, R. M. (2017). *Behave: The biology of humans at our best and worst.* Penguin.

Shapiro, G. et al., Transforming enterprises through diversity and inclusion, ILO. Geneva. Retrieved from https://policycommons.net/artifacts/2363756/transforming-enterprises-through-diversity-and-inclusion/ on 30 Mar 2023.

Sias, P. M. (2009). *Organising relationships: Traditional and emerging perspectives on workplace relationships.* Sage.

Siegel, M., H., Bradley, E., Gallo, W., & V Kasl, S. (2003). Impact of husbands' involuntary job loss on wives' mental health, among older adults. *The Journals of Gerontology, Series B, Psychological Sciences and Social Sciences.*

Smith, E. (2017). NBC orders staff to rat out misbehaving colleagues or be fired. Retrieved from https://pagesix.com/2017/12/25/nbc-tightens-sexual-harassment-rules-following-matt-lauer-mess/.

Smith, I. A., & Griffiths, A. (2022). Microaggressions, everyday discrimination, workplace incivilities, and other subtle slights at work: A meta-synthesis. *Human Resource Development Review, 21*(3), 275-299.

Snippets of Paris. (2023). French work culture: 19 differences that will astonish. Ansi Hardi SAS. Retrieved from https://snippetsofparis.com/french-work-culture/.

Steibel, D., (1997). *When talking makes things worse!* Whitehall & Norton.

Sternberg, R. J. (1986). A triangular theory of love. *Psychological review, 93*(2), 119.

Sundie, J. M., Cialdini, R. B., Griskevicius, V., & Kenrick, D. T. (2006). Evolutionary social influence. In M. Schaller, J. A. Simpson, & D. T. Kenrick (Eds.), *Evolution and social psychology* (pp. 287-316). Psychosocial Press.

Sundie, J.M., Cialdini, R.B., Griskevicius, V. & Kenrick, D.T. (2012). The world's (truly) oldest profession: Social influence in evolutionary perspective. *Social Influence, 7*(3), 134-153.

Tandoc, E. C., Tan Hui Ru, B., Lee Huei, G., Min Qi Charlyn, N., Chua, R. A., & Goh, Z. H. (2022). #CancelCulture: Examining definitions and motivations. *New Media & Society, 0*(0).

Taha, L. H., & Caldwell, B. S. (1993). Social isolation and integration in electronic environments. *Behaviour & Information Technology, 12*(5), 276-283.

Taouk, Y., Spittal, M. J., LaMontagne, A. D., & Milner, A. J. (2020). Psychosocial work stressors and risk of all-cause and coronary heart disease mortality. *Scandinavian Journal of Work, Environment & Health, 46*(1), 19-31.

The Shift Work Shop. (2022). 2022 state of sexual harassment study. Accessed from https://www.theshiftworkshop.com/2022studyaccess.

Thorson, A. R., & McBride, M. C. (2020). Self-monitoring and other non-indicators of developing a work-spouse relationship: Implications for affective organisational commitment. *International Journal of Business Communication, 60*(3), 1000-1020.

UKG. (2021). The heard and the heard-nots. Retrieved from https://workforceinstitute.org/wp-content/uploads/The-Heard-and-the-Heard-Nots.pdf.

U.S. EEOC, Integrated Mission System, Charge Data, FY 2014 – FY 2021.

Vandewal. (2007). Work spouse. Retrieved from http://everything2.com/index.pl?node_id=1878594/.

Van Eersel, J. H. W., Taris, T. W. & Boelen, P. A. (2020). Complicated grief following job loss: Risk factors for its development and maintenance. *Scandinavian Journal of Psychology, 61,* 698-706.

Waters, S. (2019). Suicide as Corporate Murder: France Télécom on Trial. *Truthout.* Retrieved from https://truthout.org/articles/suicide-as-corporate-murder-france-telecom-on-trial/.

Ward, M., May, P., Normand, C., Kenny, R.A., & Nolan, A. (2021). Mortality risk associated with combinations of loneliness and social isolation. Findings from The Irish Longitudinal Study on Ageing (TILDA). *Age and Ageing, 50*(4), 1329-1335.

Wilkie, D. (2013). Forbidden love: Workplace-romance policies now stricter. *SHRM.* Retrieved from https://www.shrm.org/resourcesand-tools/hr-topics/employee-relations/pages/forbidden-love-workplace-romance-policies-stricter.aspx.

Winstead, B. A., Derlega, V. J., Montgomery, M. J., & Pilkington, C. (1995). The quality of friendships at work and job satisfaction. *Journal of Social and Personal Relationships, 12*(2), 199-215.

Wright, S. L., & Silard, A. G. (2022). Loneliness in young adult workers. *International Journal of Environmental Research and Public Health, 19*(21), 14462.

Younger, H. R. (2023). *The art of active listening: How people at work feel heard, valued, and understood.* Berrett-Koehler.

FURTHER READING

This is a collection of sources that I did not specifically mention in the text, but I found informative, and may be helpful for readers looking to deepen their understanding of the topics of love at work and loving leadership in organisations.

Bonnavalle, N. (undated). Leading with love: Three ways leadership can show love in the workplace. Retrieved from https://www.thnk.org/blog/leading-with-love/.

Clawson, J. G. (2008). *Level three leadership: Getting below the surface* (3rd ed.). Pearson Prentice Hall.

Clifton, D. O. (2004). *How full is your bucket? Positive strategies for work and life*. Gallup Press.

Crisp, R. (2022). Slaughterhouse labour conditions create a "culture of violence," review finds. *The Guardian*.

D'Abate, C. P., & Eddy, E. R. (2007). Engaging the aging workforce: The relationship between perceived age similarity, satisfaction with coworkers, and employee engagement. *Journal of Organisational Behaviour, 28*(2), 181-196.

Damasio, A. R. (2003). *Looking for Spinoza: Joy, sorrow, and the feeling brain*. Harcourt.

DeVoe, S. E., & Iyengar, S. S. (2004). Managers' theories of subordinates: A cross-cultural examination of manager perceptions of motivation and appraisal of performance. *Organisational Behaviour and Human Decision Processes, 93*(1), 47-61.

Doshi, N., McGregor, B., & Risen, J. L. (2020). How to keep work relationships professional when everyone is remote. *Harvard Business Review.*

Eisenbeiss, S. A., Knippenberg, D. V., & Boerner, S. (2008). Transformational leadership and team innovation: Integrating team climate principles. *Journal of Applied Psychology, 93*(6), 1438-1446.

Ellemers, N., De Gilder, D., & Haslam, S. A. (2004). Motivating individuals and groups at work: A social identity perspective on leadership and group performance. *Academy of Management Review, 29*(3), 459-478.

Fernet, C., Trépanier, S. G., Austin, S., Gagné, M., & Forest, J. (2015). Transformational leadership and optimal functioning at work: On the mediating role of employees' perceived job characteristics and motivation. *Work & Stress, 29*(1), 11-31.

Fisher, B. A., & Baumeister, R. F. (2011). To belong is to matter: Sense of belonging enhances meaning in life. In P. T. P. Wong (Ed.), *The human quest for meaning: Theories, research, and applications* (2nd ed., pp. 189-204). Routledge.

Fleming, J. H., & Spicer, A. (2003). Working at a cynical distance: Implications for power, subjectivity and resistance. *Organisation Studies, 24*(7), 961-984.

Fleming, P., & Jones, M. T. (2013). *The end of corporate social responsibility: Crisis and critique.* Sage.

Ford, R., & Harding, N. (2011). The impossibility of the ethical leadership. *Business Ethics: A European Review, 20*(4), 355-366.

Ford, R., Harding, N., & Learmonth, M. (2008). *Leadership as identity: Constructions and deconstructions.* Palgrave Macmillan.

Frankl, V. E. (2006). *Man's search for meaning.* Beacon Press.

Frederickson, B. L. (2009). *Positivity: Groundbreaking research reveals how to embrace the hidden strength of positive emotions, overcome negativity, and thrive.* Crown Publishing Group.

Gardner, W. L., Fischer, D., & Hunt, J. G. (2009). Emotional labour and leadership: A threat to authenticity? *The Leadership Quarterly, 20*(3), 466-482.

George, B. (2003). *Authentic leadership: Rediscovering the secrets to creating lasting value.* Jossey-Bass.

Goffee, R., & Jones, G. (2005). Managing authenticity: The paradox of great leadership. *Harvard Business Review, 83*(12), 86-94.

Grant, A. M. (2012). Leading with meaning: Beneficiary contact, prosocial impact, and the performance effects of transformational leadership. *Academy of Management Journal, 55*(2), 458-476.

Grant, A. M., & Berry, J. W. (2011). The necessity of others is the mother of invention: Intrinsic and prosocial motivations, perspective taking, and creativity. *Academy of Management Journal, 54*(1), 73-96.

Grant, A. M., Campbell, E. M., Chen, G., Cottone, K., Lapedis, D., & Lee, K. (2007). Impact and the art of motivation maintenance: The effects of contact with beneficiaries on persistence behaviour. Organisational Behavior and Human Decision Processes, 103(1), 53-67.

Haslam, S. A., Reicher, S. D., & Platow, M. J. (2011). *The new psychology of leadership: Identity, influence and power.* Psychology Press.

Heaphy, E. D., & Dutton, J. E. (2008). Positive social interactions and the human body at work: Linking organisations and physiology. *Academy of Management Review, 33*(1), 137-162.

Herold, D. M., Fedor, D. B., Caldwell, S., & Liu, Y. (2008). The effects of transformational and change leadership on employees' commitment to a change: A multilevel study. *Journal of Applied Psychology, 93*(2), 346-357.

Hochschild, A. R. (2003). *The managed heart: Commercialisation of human feeling* (20th anniversary edition). University of California Press.

Hogan, R., Curphy, G. J., & Hogan, J. (1994). What we know about leadership: Effectiveness and personality. *American Psychologist, 49*(6), 493-504.

Hollenbeck, J. R., Gerhart, B., & Wright, P. M. (2016). Managing human resources (4th ed.). Pearson.

Hooijberg, R., & Choi, J. (2020). Unlocking the relationship between ethical leadership and creativity: The mediating role of psychological safety. *Journal of Business Ethics, 162*(1), 91-105.

Hosmer, L. T. (2011). *The ethics of management* (7th ed.). McGraw-Hill.

Ilies, R., Morgeson, F. P., & Nahrgang, J. D. (2005). Authentic leadership and eudaemonic well-being: Understanding leader-follower outcomes. *The Leadership Quarterly, 16*(3), 373-394.

Ilies, R., Nahrgang, J. D., & Morgeson, F. P. (2007). Leader-member exchange and citizenship behaviors: *A meta-analysis. Journal of Applied Psychology, 92*(1), 269-277.

Iverson, R. D., Olekalns, M., & Erwin, P. J. (1998). Affectivity, organisational stressors, and absenteeism: A causal model of burnout and its consequences. *Journal of Vocational Behavior, 52*(1), 1-23.

Jensen, M. C. (2001). Value maximisation, stakeholder theory, and the corporate objective function. *Journal of Applied Corporate Finance, 14*(3), 8-21.

Judge, T. A., Bono, J. E., Ilies, R., & Gerhardt, M. W. (2002). Personality and leadership: A qualitative and quantitative review. *Journal of Applied Psychology, 87*(4), 765-780.

Kahn, W. A. (1990). Psychological conditions of personal engagement and disengagement at work. *Academy of Management Journal, 33*(4), 692-724.

Kelloway, E. K., Barling, J., & Helleur, J. (2000). Enhancing transformational leadership: The roles of training and feedback. *Leadership & Organisation Development Journal, 21*(3), 145-149.

Kim, S., & Beehr, T. A. (2018). Self-efficacy and psychological ownership mediate the effects of empowering leadership on both good and bad employee behaviors. *Journal of Leadership & Organisational Studies, 25*(2), 157-172.

Kraimer, M. L., Seibert, S. E., Wayne, S. J., Liden, R. C., & Bravo, J. (2011). Antecedents and outcomes of organisational support for development: The critical role of career opportunities. *Journal of Applied Psychology, 96*(3), 485-500.

Lam, C. F., & Mayer, D. M. (2014). When do employees stop helping coworkers? The effects of leader-member exchange and perceived reciprocal obligation on employee lateral helping. *Journal of Applied Psychology, 99*(3), 572-588.

Lanaj, K., Johnson, R. E., & Lee, S. M. (2016). Benefits of transformational behaviors for leaders: A daily investigation of leader behaviors and need satisfaction. *Journal of Applied Psychology, 101*(2), 237-251.

Langfred, C. W. (2004). Too much of a good thing? Negative effects of high trust and individual autonomy in self-managing teams. *Academy of Management Journal, 47*(3), 385-399.

Larsson, G., & Vinberg, S. (2010). Affectivity, the Big Five, and work motivation. *European Journal of Work and Organisational Psychology, 19*(6), 628-653.

Lawler, E. E., & Rhode, J. G. (1976). Information and control in organisations. *Sloan Management Review, 17*(1), 1-12.

Lawler, E. E., & Suttle, J. L. (1972). A causal correlational analysis of the impact of satisfaction and frustration on organisational performance. *Administrative Science Quarterly, 17*(2), 229-236.

Lee, K., Carswell, J. J., & Allen, N. J. (2000). A meta-analytic review of occupational commitment: Relations with person- and work-related variables. *Journal of Applied Psychology, 85*(5), 799-811.

Leroy, H., Palanski, M. E., & Simons, T. (2012). Authentic leadership and behavioral integrity as drivers of follower commitment and performance. *Journal of Business Ethics, 107*(3), 255-264.

Liden, R. C., Wayne, S. J., Zhao, H., & Henderson, D. (2008). Servant leadership: Development of a multidimensional measure and multilevel assessment. *The Leadership Quarterly, 19*(2), 161-177.

Lindsay, D. R. (2011). Demystifying the emotional labour of leadership: Exploring the heart, head, and hands of positive and negative leadership experiences. *The Leadership Quarterly, 22*(2), 233-247.

Lowe, K. B., Kroeck, K. G., & Sivasubramaniam, N. (1996). Effectiveness correlates of transformational and transactional leadership: A meta-analytic review of the MLQ literature. *The Leadership Quarterly, 7*(3), 385-425.

Luthans, F., Youssef, C. M., & Avolio, B. J. (2007). *Psychological capital: Developing the human competitive edge.* Oxford University Press.

Macey, W. H., & Schneider, B. (2008). The meaning of employee engagement. *Industrial and Organisational Psychology, 1*(1), 3-30.

Majid, A. H. A., Yusoff, Y. M., & Hashim, H. (2017). Ethical leadership and employee silence: The mediating role of ethical culture. *Journal of Management Development, 36*(5), 618-628.

Mann, S. (1999). Emotion at work: To what extent are we expressing, suppressing, or faking it? *European Journal of Work and Organisational Psychology, 8*(3), 365-369.

Martinko, M. J., & Gardner, W. L. (1987). Learned helplessness: An alternative explanation for performance deficits. *Academy of Management Review, 12*(3), 488-495.

Maslach, C., & Leiter, M. P. (2008). Early predictors of job burnout and engagement. *Journal of Applied Psychology, 93*(3), 498-512.

May, D. R., Gilson, R. L., & Harter, L. M. (2004). The psychological conditions of meaningfulness, safety and availability and the engagement of the human spirit at work. *Journal of Occupational and Organisational Psychology, 77*(1), 11-37.

Mayer, D. M., Kuenzi, M., & Greenbaum, R. L. (2010). Examining the link between ethical leadership and employee misconduct: The mediating role of ethical climate. *Journal of Business Ethics, 95*(1), 7-16.

Meglino, B. M., Ravlin, E. C., & Adkins, C. L. (1989). A work values approach to corporate culture: A field test of the value congruence process and its relationship to individual outcomes. *Journal of Applied Psychology, 74*(3), 424-432.

Meyer, J. P., & Allen, N. J. (1990). The measurement and antecedents of affective, continuance and normative commitment to the organisation. *Journal of Occupational Psychology, 63*(1), 1-18.

Meyer, J. P., & Allen, N. J. (1991). A three-component conceptualisation of organisational commitment. *Human Resource Management Review, 1*(1), 61-89.

Meyer, J. P., & Herscovitch, L. (2001). Commitment in the workplace: Toward a general model. *Human Resource Management Review, 11*(3), 299-326.

Meyer, J. P., Paunonen, S. V., Gellatly, I. R., Goffin, R. D., & Jackson, D. N. (1989). Organisational commitment and job performance: It's the nature of the commitment that counts. *Journal of Applied Psychology, 74*(1), 152-156.

Meyer, J. P., Stanley, D. J., Herscovitch, L., & Topolnytsky, L. (2002). Affective, continuance, and normative commitment to the organisation: A meta-analysis of antecedents, correlates, and consequences. *Journal of Vocational Behavior, 61*(1), 20-52.

Meyer, J. P., Stanley, D. J., & Parfyonova, N. M. (2012). Employee commitment in context: The nature and implication of commitment profiles. *Journal of Vocational Behavior, 80*(1), 1-16.

Michie, S., & Gooty, J. (2005). Values, emotions, and authenticity: Will the real leader please stand up? *The Leadership Quarterly, 16*(3), 441-457.

Mikulincer, M., & Shaver, P. R. (2007). *Attachment in adulthood: Structure, dynamics, and change.* Guilford Press.

Milliman, J., Czaplewski, A. J., & Ferguson, J. (2003). Workplace spirituality and employee work attitudes: An exploratory empirical assessment. *Journal of Organisational Change Management,* 16(4), 426-447.

Mintzberg, H. (1973). *The nature of managerial work.* Harper & Row.

Mishra, A. K., & Spreitzer, G. M. (1998). Explaining how survivors respond to downsizing: The roles of trust, empowerment, justice, and work redesign. *Academy of Management Review, 23*(3), 567-588.

Mowday, R. T., Porter, L. W., & Steers, R. M. (1982). *Employee-organisation linkages: The psychology of commitment, absenteeism, and turnover.* Academic Press.

Mumford, M. D., Scott, G. M., Gaddis, B., & Strange, J. M. (2002). Leading creative people: Orchestrating expertise and relationships. *The Leadership Quarterly, 13*(6), 705-750.

Nahapiet, J., & Ghoshal, S. (1998). Social capital, intellectual capital, and the organisational advantage. *Academy of Management Review, 23*(2), 242-266.

Nelson, D. L., & Cooper, C. L. (2007). *Positive organisational Behavior.* Sage Publications.

Nemeth, C. J., & Staw, B. M. (1989). The tradeoffs of social control and innovation in groups and organisations. *Advances in Experimental Social Psychology, 22,* 175-210.

Neubert, M. J., Kacmar, K. M., Carlson, D. S., Chonko, L. B., & Roberts, J. A. (2008). Regulatory focus as a mediator of the influence of initiating structure and servant leadership on employee behaviour. *Journal of Applied Psychology, 93*(6), 1220-1233.

O'Reilly, C. A., III, & Chatman, J. (1986). Organisational commitment and psychological attachment: The effects of compliance, identification, and internalisation on prosocial behaviour. *Journal of Applied Psychology, 71*(3), 492-499.

O'Reilly, C. A., III, Chatman, J., & Caldwell, D. F. (1991). People and organisational culture: A profile comparison approach to assessing person-organisation fit. *Academy of Management Journal, 34*(3), 487-516.

Organ, D. W., & Ryan, K. (1995). A meta-analytic review of attitudinal and dispositional predictors of organisational citizenship behaviour. *Personnel Psychology, 48*(4), 775-802.

Podsakoff, P. M., MacKenzie, S. B., & Bommer, W. H. (1996). Transformational leader behaviors and substitutes for leadership as determinants of employee satisfaction, commitment, trust, and organisational citizenship behaviors. *Journal of Management, 22*(2), 259-298.

Podsakoff, P. M., MacKenzie, S. B., Paine, J. B., & Bachrach, D. G. (2000). Organisational citizenship behaviors: A critical review of the theoretical and empirical literature and suggestions for future research. *Journal of Management, 26*(3), 513-563.

Raghuram, S., & Arvey, R. D. (1995). Antecedents and consequences of sexual harassment in organisations: A test of an integrated model. *Journal of Applied Psychology, 80*(6), 709-723.

Riketta, M., & Van Dick, R. (2005). Foci of attachment in organisations: A meta-analytic comparison of the strength and correlates of work-group versus organisational identification and commitment. *Journal of Vocational Behavior, 67*(3), 490-510.

Rousseau, D. M. (1989). Psychological and implied contracts in organisations. *Employee Responsibilities and Rights Journal, 2*(2), 121-139.

Rousseau, D. M. (1995). *Psychological contracts in organisations: Understanding written and unwritten agreements.* Sage Publications.

Rousseau, D. M., Sitkin, S. B., Burt, R. S., & Camerer, C. (1998). Not so different after all: A cross-discipline view of trust. *Academy of Management Review, 23*(3), 393-404.

Ryan, R. M., & Deci, E. L. (2000). Self-determination theory and the facilitation of intrinsic motivation, social development, and well-being. *American Psychologist, 55*(1), 68-78.

Schaubroeck, J., Lam, S. S., & Peng, A. C. (2011). Cognition-based and affect-based trust as mediators of leader behaviour influences on team performance. *Journal of Applied Psychology, 96*(4), 863-871.

Schein, E. H. (1985). *Organisational culture and leadership: A dynamic view.* Jossey-Bass.

Schneider, B. (1987). The people make the place. *Personnel Psychology, 40*(3), 437-453.

Seibert, S. E., Wang, G., & Courtright, S. H. (2011). Antecedents and consequences of psychological and team empowerment in organisations: A meta-analytic review. *Journal of Applied Psychology, 96*(5), 981-1003.

Senge, P. M. (2006). *The fifth discipline: The art and practice of the learning organisation.* Currency Doubleday.

Shamir, B., House, R. J., & Arthur, M. B. (1993). The motivational effects of charismatic leadership: A self-concept based theory. *Organisation Science, 4*(4), 577-594.

Sheldon, K. M., & Kasser, T. (2008). Psychological threat and extrinsic goal striving. *Motivation and Emotion, 32*(1), 37-45.

Sims, H. P., Jr., Faraj, S., & Yun, S. (2009). When should a leader be directive or empowering? How to develop your own situational theory of leadership. *Business Horizons, 52*(2), 149-158.

Sosik, J. J., Avolio, B. J., & Kahai, S. S. (1997). Effects of leadership style and anonymity on group potency and effectiveness in a group decision support system environment. *Journal of Applied Psychology, 82*(1), 89-103.

Spreitzer, G. M. (1995). Psychological empowerment in the workplace: Dimensions, measurement, and validation. *Academy of Management Journal, 38*(5), 1442-1465.

Spreitzer, G. M., & Doneson, D. (2005). Musings on the past and future of employee empowerment. In C. L. Cooper, & R. J. Burke (Eds.), *The peak performing organisation* (pp. 179-190). Routledge.

Srivastava, A., Locke, E. A., & Bartol, K. M. (2001). Money and subjective well-being: It's not the money, it's the motives. *Journal of Personality and Social Psychology, 80*(6), 959-971.

Stajkovic, A. D., & Luthans, F. (1998). Self-efficacy and work-related performance: A meta-analysis. *Psychological Bulletin, 124*(2), 240-261.

Stanley, L. J., Meyer, J. P., & Topolnytsky, L. (2005). Employee cynicism and resistance to organisational change. *Journal of Business and Psychology, 19*(4), 429-459.

Steers, R. M., & Porter, L. W. (1991). *Motivation and work behavior* (5th ed.). McGraw-Hill.

Sternberg, R. J. (1996). *Successful intelligence: How practical and creative intelligence determine success in life.* Simon and Schuster.

Stouten, J., van Dijke, M., & Mayer, D. M. (2013). Does shared identity predict employees' helping behaviors? A meta-analytic investigation. *Journal of Applied Psychology, 98*(1), 35-65.

Sutton, R. I., & Hargadon, A. (1996). Brainstorming groups in context: Effectiveness in a product design firm. *Administrative Science Quarterly, 41*(4), 685-718.

Tichy, N. M., & Devanna, M. A. (1986). *The transformational leader.* Wiley.

Tims, M., Bakker, A. B., & Derks, D. (2013). The impact of job crafting on job demands, job resources, and well-being. *Journal of Occupational Health Psychology, 18*(2), 230-240.

Tost, L. P., Gino, F., & Larrick, R. P. (2013). When power makes others speechless: The negative impact of leader power on team performance. *Academy of Management Journal, 56*(5), 1465-1486.

Townsend, K., DeMarie, S., & Hendrickson, A. (1998). Virtual teams: Technology and the workplace of the future. *Academy of Management Executive, 12*(3), 17-29.

Trompenaars, F., & Hampden-Turner, C. (2011). *Riding the waves of culture: Understanding diversity in global business* (3rd ed.). Nicholas Brealey Publishing.

Tyler, T. R., & Blader, S. L. (2003). The group engagement model: Procedural justice, social identity, and cooperative behaviour. *Personality and Social Psychology Review, 7*(4), 349-361.

Van Knippenberg, D., & Sitkin, S. B. (2013). A critical assessment of charismatic-transformational leadership research: Back to the drawing board? *The Academy of Management Annals, 7*(1), 1-60.

Van Vugt, M., Hogan, R., & Kaiser, R. B. (2008). Leadership, followership, and evolution: Some lessons from the past. *American Psychologist, 63*(3), 182-196.

Vancouver, J. B., Thompson, C. M., Tischner, E. C., & Putka, D. J. (2002). Two studies examining the negative effect of self-efficacy on performance. *Journal of Applied Psychology, 87*(3), 506-516.

Vardi, Y., & Weitz, E. (2004). *Misbehavior in organisations: Theory, research, and management.* Lawrence Erlbaum Associates.

Waldman, D. A., Ramirez, G. G., House, R. J., & Puranam, P. (2001). Does leadership matter? CEO leadership attributes and profitability under conditions of perceived environmental uncertainty. *Academy of Management Journal, 44*(1), 134-143.

Wallace, J. C., Johnson, P. D., Mathe, K., & Paul, J. (2011). Structural and psychological empowerment climates, performance, and the moderating role of shared felt accountability: A managerial perspective. *Journal of Applied Psychology, 96*(4), 840-850.

Wang, G., Oh, I.-S., Courtright, S. H., & Colbert, A. E. (2011). Transformational leadership and performance across criteria and levels: A meta-analytic review of 25 years of research. *Group & Organisation Management, 36*(2), 223-270.

Warr, P. (2007). *Work, happiness, and unhappiness.* Lawrence Erlbaum Associates.

Weber, M. (1947). *The theory of social and economic organisation*. Free Press.

Weick, K. E. (1979). *The social psychology of organising* (2nd ed.). McGraw-Hill.

Weiss, H. M., & Cropanzano, R. (1999). Affective events theory: An updated meta-analysis. *Research in Organisational Behavior*, 21, 1-74.

Whitener, E. M. (2001). Do "high commitment" human resource practices affect employee commitment? A cross-level analysis using hierarchical linear modelling. *Journal of Management, 27*(5), 515-535.

Yammarino, F. J., & Dubinsky, A. J. (1994). Transformational leadership theory: Using levels of analysis to determine boundary conditions. *Personnel Psychology, 47*(4), 787-811.

Youssef-Morgan, C. M., & Luthans, F. (2015). Positive organisational behaviour in the workplace: The impact of hope, optimism, and resilience. *Journal of Management, 41*(5), 1335-1358.

Zaccaro, S. J., Foti, R. J., & Kenny, D. A. (1991). Self-monitoring and trait-based variance in leadership: An investigation of leader flexibility across multiple group situations. *Journal of Applied Psychology, 76*(2), 308-315.

Zander, L., & Butler, N. (2010). Leadership through the gender lens: Women and men in organisations. *Leadership & Organisation Development Journal, 31*(5), 402-423.

Zhang, Y., & Bartol, K. M. (2010). Linking empowering leadership and employee creativity: The influence of psychological empowerment, intrinsic motivation, and creative process engagement. *Academy of Management Journal, 53*(1), 107-128.

Zhu, W., Avolio, B. J., & Walumbwa, F. O. (2009). Moderating role of follower characteristics with transformational leadership and follower work engagement. *Group & Organisation Management, 34*(5), 590-619.

Zhu, W., & Akhtar, S. (2014). How transformational leadership influences follower helping behaviour: The role of trust and prosocial motivation. *Journal of Organisational Behavior, 35*(3), 373-392.

APPENDIX: THE FIRST PRINCIPLES AT A GLANCE

CHAPTER 2

FP2.1 Humans are social animals, and we need to belong to groups of people in order to survive.

FP2.2 Companies are modern forms of economic tribes.

FP2.3 Being made redundant can be fatal.

FP2.4 Workplace culture and environment have significant impacts on employee mental health.

FP2.5 What the consultant says is good for profit might be bad for people.

FP2.6 Workplace stress is on the rise, with compensation and overwork being the leading causes.

CHAPTER 3

FP3.1 Professional distance, though meant to facilitate multicultural collaboration, can inadvertently create barriers when generalised.

FP3.2 Proper distance safeguards others from our values.

FP3.3 Proper distance is unique and context-specific within each relationship.

FP3.4 Proper distance isn't standardised but depends on the communication recipient.

FP3.5 Proper distance can be clarified simply through seeking consent and responding graciously.

CHAPTER 4

FP4.1 Love, a multifaceted term, can range from preference to profound allegiance and sacrifice.

FP4.2 Love's association with sex and romance is just one of many interpretations.

FP4.3 Non-romantic love is expressed in languages like Arabic (*mahabba*) and Greek (*philia*).

FP4.4 The ingredients in love at work are:

- Emotional Connection,
- Shared Values,
- Positive Interactions,
- Physical Contact,
- Commitment,
- Transparency,
- Trust,
- Shared Experiences.

FP4.5 Psychology terms non-romantic but intimate and committed love as "companionate love."

FP4.6 People seek non-romantic love at work, desiring care without confusion.

FP4.7 Relationship intimacy grows through personal disclosure and empathetic response.

FP4.8 Dr. Corrie defines love as the willingness to reduce one's own quality of life, in order to improve another's.

CHAPTER 5

FP5.1 Connectedness evolves from feeling included, through being heard and understood, to being valued and loved.

FP5.2 Inclusion implies psychological safety and welcome.

FP5.3 Being heard involves acknowledgement of contributions.

FP5.4 Understanding is achieved when one's intentions are echoed back.

FP5.5 Value is perceived when one's voice incites change.

FP5.6 Love is felt in a mutually contributive relationship.

FP5.7 Levels of connectedness vary across individuals.

FP5.8 Connection skills can be improved.

FP5.9 Deep connections require effort to build but may break down quickly.

FP5.10 Greater connectedness equals more influence.

FP5.11 Connectedness isn't dictated by the organisational hierarchy.

CHAPTER 6

FP6.1 INCLUSION = PRESENCE + PSYCHOLOGICAL SAFETY

FP6.2 Extended isolation or marginalisation can lead to severe mental health issues or even be fatal.

FP6.3 As social beings, humans perceive social isolation as pain, due to survival needs.

FP6.4   DEI mainly focuses on ethnic and gender aspects, yet income inequality is most obvious by employees.

FP6.5   Proactive DEI approaches result in 25% higher profits compared to non-DEI peers.

FP6.6   Successful DEI implementation requires initiation from top leadership.

CHAPTER 7

FP7.1   HEARD=INCLUSION+ACKNOWLEDGEMENT

FP7.2   Sixty-three per cent of employees feel ignored by their manager, and 35% feel that their manager doesn't care about them as a person.

FP7.3   Psychological safety occurs when people feel they can speak, but feeling heard occurs when they believe someone is listening.

FP7.4   Employees who feel heard make better decisions and share more information.

FP7.5   The more time we spend talking, the less we have for listening.

CHAPTER 8

FP8.1   UNDERSTOOD = HEARD + ECHO

FP8.2   Misunderstandings at work cost our companies millions of dollars in lost profits.

FP8.3   Most employees don't feel that they are understood at work.

FP8.4   A dispute is an ongoing conflict; a disagreement can be a permanent state in a relationship.

FP8.5   Mushrooms are gross. ;-)

FP8.6 Understanding is more important than agreement.

FP8.7 You can love someone you disagree with.

FP8.8 Active listening is simply care and curiosity.

FP8.9 To understand the person you're listening to, you'll need to remove your filters and try to apply what you know of theirs.

CHAPTER 9

FP9.1 VALUED = UNDERSTOOD + MEANINGFUL CHANGE

FP9.2 People feel valued when what they communicate leads to meaningful change.

FP9.3 People most often choose goals based on survival, partnering, parenting, and having a good standing in society.

FP9.4 People allow others to influence them based on Reciprocity, Liking, Scarcity, Social proof, Authority, and Commitment / Consistency.

FP9.5 Companies whose employees feel valued have:

- 41% less absenteeism,
- Between 24% and 59% less turnover,
- 21% higher profitability.

FP9.6 Seventy per cent of the variance on those benefits comes down to the relationship between an employee and their line manager.

FP9.7 Active listening for value involves care, curiosity, and listening for learning.

CHAPTER 10

FP10.1 Close relationships between employees at work are good for employee wellbeing and good for business.

FP10.2 Work-spouse relationships are on the rise; they are characterised by a close emotional bond that includes mutual trust and support, honesty, loyalty, respect … and love.

FP10.3 The intimacy in a work-spouse relationship also makes possible the highest quality of critical feedback when necessary.

FP10.4 Cross-sex relationships rarely experience any sexual tension.

FP10.5 Sex between co-workers is on the rise, but sexual harassment is in decline.

CHAPTER 11

FP11.1 Cancel culture is unlove in the form of attack.

FP11.2 There are two kinds of unlove: attack and withdrawal.

FP11.3 Ghosting is unlove in the form of withdrawal.

FP11.4 Attack and withdrawal can range from minor exclusionary behaviours all the way to violence.

FP11.5 The severity of an exclusionary behaviour can be judged by its type, intensity, duration, and intent.

FP11.6 Love confronts both attack and withdrawal with the truth and an openness to reconcile.

CHAPTER 12

FP12.1 LOVED = VALUED + RECIPROCITY / TIME

FP12.2 It is more profitable in the long term to be loved than feared in leadership.

FP12.3 Love in leadership theory is not a new thing, but it hasn't received the attention it deserves.

FP12.4 Loving Leadership is the willingness of a leader to use their available resources, including time, effort, knowledge, and emotional intimacy, to improve the quality of life for those in their care.

FP12.5 Loving leaders intentionally develop the emotional culture of their organisations.

FP12.6 Shareholder supremacy is an unloving management philosophy because it is by nature exclusive of all other stakeholder groups in an organisation.

FP12.7 People pre-dominantly give and receive love in one of five love languages: gifts, affirmation, service, time, and touch.

FIGURE GUIDE

APPENDIX B: FLIRTING@WORK

Sexual harassment is not love. It doesn't come from a place of love, and it is not a genuine expression of love. Sexual harassment is an expression of the combination of sex and power, which is sparked by attraction and initially communicated with some form of flirting. So it's outside of the scope of this book to address it specifically.

However, flirting as an expression of attraction can also come from a genuine place of love, a desire to connect, and perhaps deepen the relationship on a romantic level. All true-love workplace romances have presumably originated with the sparks of both attraction and flirting. And that, arguably, sits squarely in the frame of love at work.

So, attraction and flirting are common to both power and love as expressions of sexuality in the workplace. But how do we know which is which?

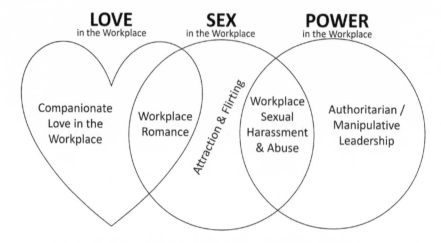

FIGURE: LOVE, SEX, AND POWER IN WORKPLACE FLIRTING

ROMANCE VS. HARASSMENT

Only the communicator knows if their flirting originates from love or power, but how can the receiver know? And what happens when the signals get crossed? The puzzle of flirting at work is challenging. Here's why…

Sexual attraction is romantic when it's mutual, but harassment if it's only one-sided.

If flirting is perceived by the receiver as coming from a place of love, then it will be interpreted as romantic (cute?), even if the attraction is not reciprocated. If flirting is perceived by the receiver as coming from a place of power, then it will be interpreted as harassment (or manipulation), even if the attraction is reciprocated.

The communicator's act of flirting may be exactly the same in both cases. It's the receiver's perception of the motive of the communicator (power or love), and the receiver's level of mutual attraction to the communicator, that determines their experience of it as either romance or harassment.

In any case, the only way to know how a person will experience flirting is to either go ahead and flirt and see what happens, or ask for consent to flirt and gather a response. Either way, it's a risk.

The receiver might mistake love for power, especially if the attraction is not reciprocated. In that case, even a loving consent request to flirt can be perceived by the receiver as harassment, especially if the communicator has hierarchical authority over the receiver in the organization.

Ultimately, this is where the hair splits. And as much as I'd like to be able to prescribe a specific set of circumstances by which we could avoid all potential for misunderstandings that occur in this very delicate and nuanced exchange, I cannot. That's why I'm calling for us to all be a more cautious in our communication, and more gracious in our responses.

[INSERT GENERAL DISCLAIMER HERE]

I don't have all of the answers, but I do have a few suggestions. I'm not a clinical psychologist, or even a manager in your place of work, so you'll have to determine for yourself if this will be useful in your particular context.

A PUNCH IN THE FACE

Asking for consent to flirt with someone is not the same as flirting with them, just as asking consent to punch someone in the face is not the same as actually punching them.

Asking is free speech, punching is assault.

Being asked by someone whether or not I would grant permission for them to punch me in the face, is not the same as them having just gone ahead and done it, even if they're stronger or more powerful than I am. However, if I view that person as stronger and more powerful than I am, I am likely to feel intimidated just the same. And although it's not illegal, it's also not loving.

Now let's say, hypothetically, that I also wanted to punch that person in the face as well, and I felt that we were perhaps equals in a fight that had been brewing for a while. I might very well invite the punch, outsourcing the starting of the fight to the other person. Then the consent request would be perfectly justified.

The only way for the puncher to know if I'm into fighting with them is for them to ask. And in that case, I should respond graciously: "No, thank you." And the same should apply to flirting.

CAUTIOUS CONSENT AND A GRACIOUS RESPONSE

The risk that's taken in a flirting exchange that comes from a genuinely good heart, is real on both sides. The communicator risks rejection, and the receiver risks feeling manipulated or harassed.

Love is powerful, but it's not simple.

Ask for consent to flirt only if your motives are genuinely romantic in nature. And don't make a second request if the first is graciously declined. The first consent request might be genuinely romantic, but the second is almost certainly harassment.

And be gracious in your responses to genuine consent requests. Remember, you can't read their minds any better than they can read yours.

And finally, perhaps save the exchange for a time when you're not in the office, just in case you've misunderstood the signals.

Start with consent to share a meal, or a drink, and see if that helps.

Good luck.

NOTES

Milton Keynes UK
Ingram Content Group UK Ltd.
UKHW041342161223
434508UK00001B/130